Throughout the world there is deep spiritual unrest and dissatisfaction with organized religions as they have come down to us. Those steeped in the spirit of science and modern thought are eagerly groping for a faith which will meet the demands of modern science and fulfil the hunger for the Unseen. Professor Radhakrishnan, who has devoted a lifetime to the study of the religious problems of the East and West, here sets forth his reflections on the religion of the future which will make for the development of a world community. The author evaluates the anti-metaphysical bias of our scientific age and interprets this outlook in positive rather than in negative terms, not as a loss of the sense of the spiritual but as a gain of the wholeness of experience. This book is written with deep religious feeling and will offer comfort to our bewildered generation, for it affirms the doubts and insecurities of modern man and points beyond them to the grounds for hope. It appreciates the intellectual difficulties of belief and gives the widest social content to religion.

RELIGION IN A CHANGING WORLD

BY THE SAME AUTHOR

The Bhagavadgita
The Brahma Sutra
East and West in Religion
The Hindu View of Life
An Idealist View of Life
Indian Philosophy
Principal Upanisads
Recovery of Faith
Religion and Society

S. RADHAKRISHNAN

RELIGION IN A CHANGING WORLD

LONDON · GEORGE ALLEN AND UNWIN LTD
NEW YORK · HUMANITIES PRESS

FIRST PUBLISHED IN 1967

PRINTED IN GREAT BRITAIN
in 12 pt Old Style type
BY C. TINLING AND CO. LTD, LIVERPOOL
LONDON AND PRESCOT

PREFACE

We are now in one of those great periods of history when humanity is taking a leap into the future and shifting its axis of conduct, national and international. The world has changed in innumerable ways in our century, much more than in the preceding 5,000 years. We are transitional figures involved in a new stage of history. The sudden widening of intellectual perspectives, the increasing secularization of life, the rapid dissolution of accepted values, are preparing men's minds and hearts for a new conception of human solidarity based on the equal rights of all human beings, whatever be their caste or class, colour or community, race or religion. The challenge posed by the breakup of traditional concepts in philosophy, politics and arts has to be met, understood and controlled. The accent of anxiety, the note of despair which we see all over the world are a call for a radical change in our views of life and ways of behaviour, for a clearer recognition of man's inherent dignity and of the brotherhood of man.

The widespread mental unhappiness is traceable to the neurosis of emptiness which is tearing asunder the world not only politically but emotionally. We are the children of our age, sceptics, unbelievers, nihilists. There is a schism in the human heart, an inner disorder, a profound fissure in our make-up. Deep down we share the religious instincts which we deny on the plane of reason. The will to believe is resisted by the pleas of reason. We need to find our way back to the living spirit which reconciles opposites. We are on the threshold of a new age of spirit.

If we are unable to discard the dead forms which still persist and to create new institutions which enshrine the new ideals, we will pass out and yield to another species; for the earth will survive the self-destructive passions of men. We have achieved sufficient knowledge to create a great civilization but not sufficient wisdom to control and preserve it. The Greek City-States, for example, more than two thousand years ago gave mankind some of its greatest philosophers, artists and dramatists. They are still a part of our heritage but all the brilliance of the Greeks could not save them, since they could not maintain peace among themselves.

Our scientific and technological achievements are of a staggering character. We are striving to touch the stars and reach the moon, yet we are clinging to established relationships among sovereign States, which, in the nuclear age, will lead to disaster. It is a desperate situation in which nations seem to be standing very much on their own at what is a turning point in our history, a crisis which heralds either a total catastrophe or a new beginning. We need courage and discipline now more than brilliance. The human individual has to be renewed if human society is to be preserved. We have to affirm the doubts and insecurities of modern men and point beyond them to the ground of hope. Man is searching for his identity, for the meaning of life, for the significance of the defeat he suffers by clinging to a reality that crumbles in his hands. Our life and literature are full of stories of agonies, disasters, ruin of whole peoples, whole nations. Ruin is a consequence of human criminality so outrageous that even the highest art cannot do justice to it. Much of the literature of our generation creates a climate of doubt and bewilderment in which the recognition of larger purposes of life is denied and the self-confidence of people is damaged. At the height of our power and technological might, we have our deepest moments of insecurity. In spite of all our advance in science and technology, we feel as never before the threat of the meaningless, the absurd. When the cries of anguish die away, these miseries, it is hoped, will serve as levers to progress, if not to universal peaceful coexistence, at least to a little more understanding, a little more strengthening of the sense of justice, a little more spreading of compassion. It is a hopeful sign that religions feel that they have a responsibility to the whole of mankind and not merely to their own adherents.

Religion has been the great force for the disciplining of man's nature but unfortunately to many people it has lost its value and validity. It is the difficulty of religious beliefs that is responsible for the present distemper of the world. We need a faith that is reasonable, a faith that we can adopt with intellectual integrity and ethical conviction, a large, flexible faith for the whole human race to which each one of the living religions can bring its specific contribution. We need a faith which demands loyalty to the whole of mankind, and not to this or that fraction of it, a faith to which the secular and emancipated mind might cling even in the face of disaster.

All living faiths are anxious for survival and are readjusting themselves to the new conditions of life. Hinduism and Buddhism are revising their social attitudes while preserving their permanent values. These religions are attempting to scrape off the crust of distortions which have accumulated over the centuries. Catholicism and Protestantism, the two dominant forms of Christianity, are revising and reappraising their policies. Pope Paul VI and the Archbishop of Canterbury signed a joint declaration on the 24th of March this year, in the Basilica of St Paul's at Rome, pledging the Roman Catholics and the Anglican Churches to work towards unity. Presbyterians, Methodists and other Churches are engaged in a dialogue. Islam, which arose in a spirit of reform against the evils of the day, is now examining whether its basic tenets are relevant to the present conditions of the world. All religions are persuaded that, if religion is to be effective, it should not be a block to rational thinking and social progress. They are not to be regarded as rigid, immutable entities impervious to each other; they are all undergoing revolutionary readjustments to modern life. All religions should have the responsibility of understanding the changes in the social order, interpreting them, preparing us to meet them, by modifying themselves when the best interests of society so dictate. We are not born into a dead world.

We must become aware of the future dimensions of human life. Man's psychological structure is evolving in ways both comparable to and radically different from those found in organic evolution. What is ahead of us is growth in our psyche.

This book is intended to be a small contribution to the development of a spiritual faith which may serve as a basis for the new world order. I have not loaded the book with much technical detail but tried to give the ordinary reader an intelligible account of religion as I see it. I hope it may be of interest to some others also.

S. R.

30th November, 1966
New Delhi

CONTENTS

CHAPTER I

THE EMERGING WORLD SOCIETY[1]

I

A new world society is gradually emerging. It is growing quietly, imperceptibly in the minds and hearts of men. The tumult and the excitement, the anger and the violence, the perplexities of spirit and the ambiguities of expression are the pangs of the birth of something new. We of this generation are called upon to work for this new order with all the strength and capacity for suffering we possess.

Only two kinds of people are happy and free from tension, the utter fool and the one who has surpassed himself, gone beyond his mind, and attained the state of wisdom. All people in between are in varying stages of tension and sorrow.[2]

When religious prophets and philosophers speak of our common humanity, of the natural kinship of human beings, it is an essential part of wisdom and a real need of the enlightened spirit. There is a wider recognition of this fact today than ever before in history. Man's basic physical structure, his mental make-up, his moral needs, his spiritual aspirations are the same the world over. The cycle of birth, growth, childhood and youth, of sickness, old age and death, of love and friendship, of sorrow and joy is the same for all men. We share a common

[1] Previously published in the Jawaharlal Nehru Memorial Volume, *The Emerging World* (1964).

[2] *yaśca mūḍhatamo loke yaśca buddheḥ paraṁ gataḥ*
tāv ubhau sukham edhete kliśyaty antarīto janaḥ.
Bhāgavata Purāṇa, III. vii. 17.

origin and a common destiny: *ekaiva mānuṣī jātiḥ.* The human race is one. This oneness of humanity is more than a phrase, it is not a mere dream. It is becoming a historic fact. With the speeding up of communications, ideas and tools now belong to man as man. The necessities of the historical process are making the world into one. We stand on the threshold of a new society, a single society. Those who are awake to the problems of the future adopt the ideal of the oneness of mankind as the guiding principle of their thought and action.

II

In previous centuries we had a limited vision of the world; of Asia, of Europe, of Africa. None of these large continents is the whole world. They have come together and cannot get away from one another. The sciences of archaeology and anthropology reveal ancient art of great achievement, of beauty and complexity which yet remained outside the traditional stream of Asian, European or African history.

Plausible generalizations are made by philosophers of history which are highly misleading. Hegel in his *Lectures on the philosophy of History* says that 'Persia is the land of light, Greece the land of grace, India the land of dream, Rome the land of empire.'[1] It is true of all cultures that the greatest gift of life is the dream of a higher life. The pursuit of perfection has been the dominating motive of human life. Man is essentially a remaker. He is not content with the patterns of the past.

[1] E.T. by Sibree (1861).

East and West are relative terms. They are geographical expressions and do not represent cultural types. The differences among countries like China, Japan and India are quite as significant as those among European or American countries. Specific cultural patterns with distinctive beliefs and habits developed in different regions in relative isolation from one another. There were periods when China and India were pre-eminent in cultural affairs; others became prominent when Western nations were filled with the urge to expand. For the last three centuries, Western nations aided by scientific development have dominated the East. The scientific and the industrial developments of the past three centuries have created a great gulf not only between the East and the West but between the present Western civilization and that of its own past.

Recent developments have given rise to the misleading impression that, while the West is scientific in outlook, the East is spiritually minded. The one is said to be rational, while the other is held to be religious. The one is regarded as dynamic and perpetually changing, while the other is treated as static and unchanging. If we take a long view, we will find that China and India have made fundamental contributions to science and technology till three or four hundred years ago, and there have been illustrious examples of religious wisdom and sanctity in the West. The more we understand one another the more we feel that we are like one another. East and West do not represent two different types of consciousness or modes of thought.

Science and religion are aspects of every culture.

The rational and the spiritual are two strands inextricably woven in human nature, though in varied patterns. One or the other may be more prominent in different periods of human history.

Human beings are fundamentally the same and hold the same deep values. The differences among them which are, no doubt, significant, are related to external, temporary and social conditions and are alterable with them.

III

In spite of sharp international conflicts, setbacks and mutual slandering, the world is getting to be one. Science knows no barriers. Art and culture are becoming common possessions. The isolated existence of human groups has become outdated. It is just a matter of hours to travel from one end of the world to another. Radio, television, and the press help us to follow events in other countries. Physical barriers have broken down, preparing the way for intellectual communication and spiritual communion. The most distant states have become near neighbours and an international society is in prospect.

The world is drawn together by the interconnectedness of world economy. Nations in Asia and Africa are passing through what is called a revolution of rising and yet unfulfilled demand for more reasonable standards of life. They are treading the road to modernization which is another name for industrialization. We are all using the same language in science and employing the same tools for industrial development. As a result, new sets of values are springing up everywhere. Never before have men had the means of communication or the bonds of interdependence through which a world community is rendered possible. The world has become a unit and demands that it should be treated as one.

Today this is not only possible but necessary in view of the development of nuclear weapons of fantastic power. Leaders of States talk of the development of inter-continental ballistic missiles, the incomparable fire power they possess and the eventual obliteration of any possible aggressor from the face of the earth. A nuclear arms race indicates the possibility, if not the probability, of putting an end in a war to the human species. It is not a question of who is the world's strongest military power or who has the lead in inter-continental missiles. Whoever may be the mightier power, no one will survive a nuclear war. It is a dangerous illusion to believe that the use of these weapons will result in a decisive advantage to those who possess them. There is no such thing as military invincibility. Nuclear war will mean the ruin of all. The fate of all nations is inseparably tied up. Either we live together or die together. It is either one society or no society.

IV

The ending of the human adventure on earth is a possibility we have to reckon with. Faced by such a challenge, our differences of race and religion, class or colour, nation and ideology, become irrelevant. We have to devise a realistic way by which humanity does not compass its own destruction.

In the present condition of the world with its nervous apprehension, it is essential and urgent for us to adjust ourselves to the new realities and to adopt measures to prevent the use of the new formidable means of destruction. We should develop a new flexibility, new powers of creative adaptation.

Militarism and nationalism have become outdated, outmoded. Heracleitus spoke of war as the father of all changes. For centuries, war has been used as a method for settling international disputes. It has been terrible in its consequences. It has wiped out whole civilizations and destroyed entire peoples. But the new weapons have completely changed the nature of warfare and made it devastating in its consequences. If a general agreement is not reached, if mutual confidence is not restored, if competition in this lethal race goes on, we will live in a very precarious way, with the sentence of death threatening us all. War in the present age means the suicide and not the survival of man. As a method of settling international disputes, war has to be abandoned. There is no alternative to peace.

In mankind's chequered history we have fought each other again and again to uphold our distinctive ways of life. The instinct for each to cling to his own way is adopted by the nation State at the present level of human evolution. Nationalism is a collective form of selfishness. Each race, each creed, each nation regards itself as the chosen of God, as the elect of the future, as the educator of the human race. There is a selfrighteousness which each nation adopts about its culture, its pattern of life and unconsciously, if not consciously, it uses its reason to serve its emotions and develop an aggressive hostility to all those who reject this pattern and are committed to other ways of life. We deride what we do not understand; we reject what we do not recognize. National arrogance is a characteristic of all nations, in the East as in the West. The ancient Greeks destroyed the great civilization they developed by their passionate and violent attachment to their States.[1] La Fontaine distinguished Frenchmen from the Spaniards by referring to national pride, that 'ours is much more stupid and theirs much more mad.' A Frenchman declared that English is simply French badly spelt and badly pronounced. When national leaders use the apparatus of modern technology, such as the radio and television, they tell their peoples that they are dishonoured by defeat, that they are threatened by their neighbours, that they should dare all things and die, if necessary, for the glory of their fatherland or mother country or ideological pattern. The barriers that separate peoples are thus intensified.

The responsibility of literary writers and historians is great in the matter of exaggerating past wrongs and keeping old sores running. They help to make nations drunk by imparting to them false memories, inducing in them a sense of cosmic destiny. While, as individual human beings, we are sensible, humble, generous and appreciative of others, as members of this or that nation State, we are bitter, arrogant, vain and almost unbearable.

Nation States are too narrow for the modern world, where we have conquered space and can move faster than sound. Gāndhi, even when he

[1] *cf.* Tibullus: "O Rome, thy name is fated to rule the earth."

was fighting for India's independence, warned us against the reactionary character of nationalism. He said, 'A fallen and prostrate India cannot be of help to herself or the world. A free and enlightened India can be of help to herself and the world. I want my country to be free that one day, if need be, she may die that humanity may live.' It is in self-surrender that we fortify ourselves. Nations, like individuals, become great not by what they acquire but by what they renounce.

Nations are not immortal. They are not the permanent possessors of this planet. They are its temporary tenants. They will last long if they adhere to the moral law. The doom of nations cannot be long delayed if the cupidities of men persist. Nations aim at permanence. We know, however, that all great societies perished leaving behind the heritage of arts and skills, ideas and ideals, on which we still build. No society dies in vain. All living things die but out of death comes life.

Gāndhi required us to be faithful to the inner voice of conscience, the divine law not written by the hand of man but inflexible none the less, the eternal fountain source of all the codes that have ever been written in the course of ages. It is this moral law that binds the members of the human family together, and gives them a new sense of responsibility for the safety and happiness of the whole human family. By being ourselves, we best serve the interests of others. The interdependence of nations has become so close that no nation can be hurt without injury to the rest. Nations are no more islands; frontiers are losing their significance.

Belief in co-existence is not the outcome of expediency or of weakness. It is the only way to rid the world of exclusiveness, intolerance and misunderstanding. There are no more closed societies. The new order we seek is not either national or continental. It is neither eastern nor western. It is universal. We must develop a sense of perspective and realize that our nation is one of many, and each makes a specific contribution to the richness and variety of the world. Humanity is not this race or that nation, but the whole of mankind which is getting together, we hope, for purposes of co-operation. Simply because war has been with us for many centuries, it does not follow that it will continue to be with us for all time.[1]

There is a conflict between the old concept of the nation state, separate, sovereign, absolute, autonomous and the new international community where we have to work together if we are to survive. It is time we abandon the past with national sovereignty and faith in force, and work for the future with its ideals of peace, freedom and justice under law. History is a road in which vital points are crossroads.

[1] Some years ago the then Soviet Premier, Mr Khrushchev, said at Bucharest that 'Lenin's dictum that war is inevitable between the capitalist and the socialist groups is outdated in the present nuclear age'. 'The Communists are realistically minded people. They realise that in the current situation the relations between the two world systems should be built in such a way as to preclude the possibility of war.' Again, 'to prevent war, including local war, because it can develop into a world war, every people should bring pressure to bear on its government, to compel it to abide by the principles of peaceful co-existence of States with different social systems'. Mr Khrushchev thought that the old doctrine of the inevitability of conflict between capitalism and socialism had no meaning today. Later, on the anniversary of Lenin's birth, Mr Khrushchev said 'one must not fail to note the emergence of mighty forces which act against war'.

V

Past history of human evolution gives us the hope that by intelligent planning and deliberate effort, we may slowly give up the military method of settling disputes. Within the nation, we do not ordinarily resort to force to assert our rights. We have established the rule of law and we strive to settle our disputes through resort to law or by other peaceful methods.

There are individuals who are tempted to take the law into their own hands, and we use the police force to deter them from the use of lawless violence. This secures that no one uses force to gain his selfish ends. Within a nation, we have the rule of law, the framework of justice and a police force.

We also establish conditions of human welfare, which do not encourage unrest, disorder and strife. Laws within nations are broken when legitimate ambitions are thwarted, when misery is widespread and the future seems blocked. When whole groups feel that they have no chance of maintaining themselves decently, they rebel against the established order. The forces of social passion, humane concern and compassion are at work within the nation and seek to maintain a healthy condition in society.

All those, who belong to a nation, share certain ideals and purposes, and work for the general welfare of the community as a whole. A nation is not a casual association of men for the performance of certain specific functions. It is a vital union. The sense of nationality is derived not from race, language or religion, but from traditional values accepted by the members of the nation. They have a sense of honour, and respect for indefinable obligations and intangible values.

If conditions which prevail within a welfare state are extended on a world scale, we should be prepared for a little sacrifice of national sovereignty, and be willing to accept peaceful methods of settling disputes, enforce peaceful legal solutions and avert violence, secure minimum economic conditions of well-being, and remove the grievances of large communities which suffer from political subjection and racial oppression and develop a moral community based on spiritual values. A proper appreciation of the duties and responsibilities implied in world citizenship is necessary today. We have to lift the world off its hinges and transform the national man into a universal man.

The United Nations Organisation is the first step towards the creation of an authoritative world order. It has not got the power to enforce the rule of law. It has used, on occasions, military force. There is discussion about disarmament, inspection and control. The cold war is the result of the two power blocs facing each other in Europe, Asia and Africa. If the cold war is to end, the groups should abandon the armament race to annihilation. If the two sides seek, all the time, arms that would outmatch those of each other, and suspect and distrust each other, war becomes inevitable. Even as national welfare requires us to give up the personal right to use force, international security requires the surrender of the right to use force on the part of nations. We should strive to get the weapons out of the hands of nations and put them in international keeping. Except for local police forces, the world's arms should be in the hands of an international authority.

We need an international code of justice which should be enforced impartially. All this is possible only if there is general, simultaneous, controlled disarmament and the parallel establishment of an international police force.

If agreement is reached on total and universal disarmament, setting free large funds, these funds can be used for rendering extensive aid to all the under-developed nations. The World Health Organization, the International Labour Organization, the Food and Agriculture Organization, the World Bank and the Children's Fund and such other agencies are attempting to correct the present inequalities of opportunity and living standards, among the nations of the world. They recognize that the economic problems are common to all humanity, irrespective of race, culture or nationality. Hunger knows no nationality. Despair is not peculiar to any people. The world's resources should be developed for the benefit of all mankind. It is increasingly recognized that favoured nations have a responsibility to raise the less favoured ones to a higher level. Peace is secure only if the people of the world are freed from the burden of armaments, and from hunger, destitution, disease and despair.

Colonialism and racial discrimination are admitted to be the sources of major conflicts and require to be eliminated. Provision should be made for peaceful changes towards the political freedom and economic well-being of backward nations.

The sense of belonging together to the same nation is derived from a sense of sharing the same memories and hopes, the same historical experiences, the same artistic and cultural heritage. If membership of one world is to be developed, projects like the East–West understanding and co-operation should help us to realize the cultural wealth and knowledge to which we are all heirs. When mischievous misunderstanding is at work, it is our duty to work for creative understanding among nations.

It is for the world leaders to determine the practical steps by which the sources of power and communication now available to us can be used for closer co-operation and friendliness among the peoples of the world. No political understanding can be permanent, without understanding at the cultural level. Apart from its intrinsic importance, such understanding contributes to the enrichment of human experience. Science and industry, education and culture are unifying us at the physical and intellectual levels. We need to look upon humanity, not as a mere organization but as a living organism united from within, by those values which are inseparable from human dignity and freedom. When the sense of human community is lacking, society becomes a riotous mob.

We cannot conceive of a world without national differences, without cultural variety and artistic wealth. In a world which is becoming standardized, variety of cultures imparts beauty and creativeness. It is for organizations like the UNESCO to develop in the minds of men that large, inclusive vision of humanity through understanding and respect for differences, and to increase global awareness and co-operation in the ways of peace. The world community will have, in common, science and technology, economic arrangements and political forms; but it will also help the varied peoples of the world to develop their local customs, arts and literature. These will save the new civilization from drabness and monotony. Diversity is an essential factor of community.

VI

We stand on the edge of one of the most exciting periods of human history. Modern science and technology contain the promise and peril of the modern age. The opportunities that lie ahead of us are unique. Scientific developments have placed such tools and instruments in our hands, that we can secure the good life for all. The new sources of energy may be used to transform agriculture, industry and transport. We can raise the standards of people all over the world by the employment of atomic energy. We can dredge the seas, melt the rocks, make deserts blossom and produce abundance for all.

Communications have opened up opportunities for the communion of human minds. Civilizations meet and confront each other, fertilize each other, illumine each other. The vital elements of civilizations, prayer and worship, learning and scholarship, vision and understanding, beauty and art are as real and effective as suspicions and jealousies, hatreds and rivalries. We should grasp the opportunities offered to us, and not throw them away in a blind love for rigid historical positions. We should get rid of the old idolatries, and develop a sense of moral community and create institutions which express our common purposes.

Mankind is on trial. In these days of deepening cleavages between different ways of life and growing anxiety for the future, we have to invoke the highest aspirations of mankind for easing tensions, and understanding each other's ways of life. In spite of the troublous days in which we live, man can raise himself above himself, above the constricting conditions of life. To be mistaken and yet be compelled to go on believing, what one's innermost being tells one is wrong, that is the tragedy of man. No external reform will reach the heart of the problem. The spirit of man has to be converted to the truth of our new conditions. We have to labour with the souls of men. Betterment must begin with the individual. We must show our preparedness to live together in confidence and friendship. We must uphold the conviction that there are no chosen races, creeds or nations, and that we all have the blessing of God, if we behave properly. What we need is a change of heart which religion can effect.

The obstacle which stands in the way of the achievement of the new world, the one world, is not the lack of material resources or intellectual power but simple cussedness; it is greed, vanity, the desire for prestige and honour. We cling to the belief that our way of life is the right one, and it will win. In our passion to make our cause win, we excuse everything which is cruel and unjust in the behaviour of our own group. There is no attempt to get over things which we know and feel to be bad. It is wrong to assume that actions of a nation are not to be judged by standards of morality. Public opinion takes success and expediency as the test of group action. The German writer, Herder, expresses his central conviction in these striking words:

'To brag of one's country is the stupidest form of boastfulness. A nation is a wild garden full of bad plants and good, vices and follies mingle with virtues and merit. What Don Quixote will break a lance for this Dulcines?'

We may have an innocent attachment to our family, city and language, but aggressive nationalism is detestable in all its manifestations, and wars are mere crimes. It is the sacred egoism of nations that has led to disasters.

The human spirit has contradictory elements, of grandeur and pettiness, generosity and meanness, nobility and fury, courage and cowardice. Man is too vain, too stupid to know himself. He is so self-loving that he endures in himself the faults which he cannot stand in others. With stupidity, even the gods fight in vain. The mounting tensions are the result of a black, blind, uncontrolled fury. Danger exerts a powerful fascination. It is like the condition of vertigo, in which the wild temptation to plunge is heightened by the terror of the abyss. When we think of the race in nuclear armaments, we feel that we are preparing ourselves with a suicidal violence for destroying life, for making the world break into fragments.

Human life has a double character. Man is said to be 'a little less than God' and also 'a beast that perishes'. These conflicting descriptions come from the *Psalms*. One psalmist says:

'Thou hast made him a little less than God
And dost crown him with glory and honour.'

Another adds:

> 'Man cannot abide in his pomp,
> He is like the beasts that perish.'

Man is both these things, a spirit-centred being, a little less than God and a human animal like the beasts that perish. He is a frail creature at the mercy of the relentless, unheeding powers of nature. He is also a being with his unique worth and dignity. He is now a split personality. Neurosis is an inner cleavage, the state of being at war with oneself. Each individual seems to consist of two persons opposed to each other. Faust says: 'two souls, alas, dwell in my breast apart'. Freud speaks of the two basic instincts:

> 'After long doubts and vacillations we have decided to assume the existence of only two basic instincts, *Eros* and the *destructive instinct*. The aim of the first of these basic instincts is to establish even greater unities and to preserve them thus—in short, to bind together; the aim of the second, on the contrary, is to undo connections and so to destroy things . . . For this reason we also call it the *death instinct*.'[1]

Life is a perpetual struggle between good and evil. Our minds oscillate between groundless optimism, when we overlook evil, and pointless despair, when we overlook good. The most difficult problem is self-control. Science has given us enormous control over non-human nature, but science does not help us to control our own nature. Unless man grows in his spiritual character in

[1] *An Outline of Psycho-analysis*, E.T. by James Strachey (1949), pp. 5–6.

proportion to his gigantic technological stature, the future will be in danger. The great problems of humanity cannot be solved by general laws but only through the regeneration of attitudes of individuals. Each one should try to overthrow the old order within oneself. Each one requires to be renewed. Every triumph of human devotion and spiritual energy raises our world to a higher level, and brings it nearer the goal of unity, of freedom. Man's pilgrimage cannot stop, until justice and love hold sway over the lives of men.

The human condition has to be changed. Instead of wasting our energies in patching up the ailments of existing institutions, we should try to create new institutions through changes in ourselves.

Man's ability to change his nature is impeded today more than ever before by the hold of the group on him. Modern man is lost in the crowd to an extent which is pathological. The disease of conformity is what we suffer from. There is no time for independent reflection. We accept the views which are furnished to us by our society. Our nationality, our race, our creed, our political affiliations, what they dictate is treated as exempt from criticism. By this attitude, truth suffers as much as our intellectual integrity does. It is by resisting such methods of conformism, that we abolished slavery, torture and other forms of inhumanity. Man's concern for his own awareness and for every human being should not be stifled. The anti-rational attitude is common to all established institutions and organizations. Uniformity is a greater danger than disunity. Doubt and enquiry are more helpful to the development of the individual than regimented thought. We should seek unity, not by the suppression of thought, but through thought. Under the pressure of authority and propaganda, it is difficult for us to develop an independent thoughtful approach to life's problems.

The impulse to perfection is innate in man. We naturally seek to raise ourselves to a higher degree of value. We wish to wake people up from thoughtlessness to a new spirit of humanity. We are makers of history. We may be threatened by disaster; yet we should resist. We should stand by the side of those who choose life rather than by those who wish to destroy. We cannot be content with the past. Every morning brings a new day and every pulse beat a new life.

CHAPTER II

THE RELIGIOUS PREDICAMENT

I

Religions have helped us to realize that there is more to life than the satisfaction of immediate needs of hunger, sex, sleep. They have given us support to our values, and helped us to harmonize our dreams and wishes.

When religions were first formulated, there was not much difficulty in accepting the validity of miracles and dogmas. Even as ancient mythologies disappeared, the unscientific dogmas, it is said, will fade out. Since they die hard, we are ill at ease. Greater demands are made on present day men than were ever made on people living in earlier times.[1]

Eastern religions like Hinduism and Buddhism seek to base their beliefs on observed data and hold that the two sides of man's nature, the rational and the spiritual, should work together. Though

[1] 'For them there was no difficulty at all in believing in the virgin birth of the hero and demi-god, and Justin Martyr was still able to use this argument in his *Apology*. Nor was the idea of a redeeming god-man anything unheard of, since practically all Asiatic potentates together with the Roman Emperor were of a divine nature. But we have no further use even for the divine right of kings! The miraculous tales in the gospels, which easily convinced people in those days, would be a *petra-scandali* in any modern biography, and would evoke the very reverse of belief—*Hermes ter unus* Hermes thrice one was not an intellectual absurdity but a philosophical truth. On these foundations the dogma of Trinity could be built up convincingly. For modern man this dogma is either an impenetrable mystery or an historical curiosity, preferably the latter.'

The Collected Works of C. G. Jung, Vol. IX, Part II (1959), p. 177.

they also speak of such things as miracles, they do not belong to the core of these religions.

In the West, the development of religion has been struggling to come to terms with the spirit of reason. Greek thought had faith in reason and the rationality of the world. The Greeks felt that the world made sense. In later times, scientific developments disturbed faith in traditional beliefs. Geologists pushed the origin of the earth far beyond the time assigned by religions. The evolution of human life was traced by biologists to the caves and jungles. The astronomers shook the picture of our planet as the centre of the universe. The earth from being the centre of the universe was reduced to the position of a star among stars. Galileo transformed man's view of the universe. Copernicus presented the first major conflict between religion and science. Luther condemned Copernicus outright. 'This fool,' Luther said, 'wished to reverse the entire science of astronomy, but sacred scripture tells us that Joshua commanded the sun to stand still, and not the earth.' The elevation of the inerrancy of scripture to the level of dogma, led to considerable intellectual questioning.

Primitive science was animistic and there was a revival of animistic science in the period of the Renaissance. In the first half of the seventeenth century, rationalistic philosophy and naturalistic science triumphed. With Descartes human reason became supreme, and a mechanistic view of the world developed. Laplace told Napoleon that there was no need for the hypothesis of God in his system. Matter regarded as rigid and immutable entities is resolved into energy by the relativity theory and the principle of uncertainty. Reality is found in the realm of relationships. Ultimate questions like death and sin do not call for anything transcendent. God is incredible and dispensable, and emotionally he is superfluous. If anything, God is a dangerous illusion which prevents us from facing realities and shouldering responsibility. He is neither a refuge nor a compensation for miseries, which we should fight by our own effort. Scepticism and a moral passion for betterment are enough for many.

The debate between science and religion is not limited to particular questions of scientific fact or history. It has also to reckon with the general feeling, that science has made religion out of date, for the spirit of science is essentially empirical, while the realities with which religion deals are said to be outside experience altogether. We are called upon to admit scientific knowledge of experienced data and not of non-empirical or supernatural objects.

Criticism of religion and its history and the study of other religions are leading to a re-examination of the sources and validity of accepted views. Many historical critics today affirm that 'we can know almost nothing concerning the life and personality of Jesus.[1] Professor R. H. Lightfoot says: 'it seems then that the form of the earthly no less than of the heavenly Christ is for the most part hidden from us.' 'To practise Christology,' says Professor Tillich, 'does not mean to turn backwards to an unknown historical past, or to exert oneself about the applicability of questionable mythical categories to an unknown

[1] Professor Rudolf Bultmann. See H. J. Paton: *The Modern Predicament* (1955), pp. 227–8.

historical personality.' Even such an orthodox theologian like Karl Barth observes:

'Jesus Christ, in fact, is also the Rabbi of Nazareth, historically so difficult to get information about, and when it is obtained is apt to impress us as a little commonplace alongside more than any other founder of a religion and even alongside many later representatives of his own religion.'

Emil Brunner says: 'Faith presupposes as a matter of course, *a priori* that the Jesus of history is not the same as the Christ of faith.'[1] Jesus who died at Jerusalem is not the same as the Christ who lives and reigns.[2] Dietrich Bonhoeffer tells us that the Church must come out of its stagnation. He complains that:

'our Church, which in these years has fought only for its self-preservation, as if it were an end in itself, is incapable of being the bearer of the personal and redeeming word for mankind. For this reason earlier words must become powerless. Yet the day will come on which people will again be called upon to pronounce the word of

[1] 'But the truth is, it is not Jesus as historically known, but Jesus as spiritually arisen within men, who is significant for our time and can help it. Not the historical Jesus but the spirit which goes forth from Him and in the spirits of men strives for new influence and rule is that which overcomes the world.'

(Schweitzer.)

[2] 'To speak as if Jesus were in any way identical with God the Father would be to fall into a grievous error which the Church through all its early controversies refused to tolerate. But to speak as if Jesus could ever occupy the central place in Christian faith apart from His revelation of the Father . . . would be to fall into another grievous error. . . . The object of Christian faith is neither God apart from Christ, nor God and Christ, but God in Christ.'

(D. Baillie.)

God in such a way that the world will be changed and renewed by it. There will be a new language, perhaps quite unreligious, but liberating and elevating as the language of Jesus.'[3]

Anyway, at a time of serious questioning, religion cannot be based on an appeal to historical facts.

Historical research has been revolutionizing our understanding of the Old and New Testaments. From the discovery of the Dead Sea Scrolls in 1947, it is clear that Christian doctrine developed from Jewish sectarianism. There were several sects on the fringe of Judaism. Among the most important were the Zadokites, the Zealots and the Essenes. It has long been believed that Christianity had its roots in the latter group. But the main source of our knowledge of the Essenes was the Jewish historian, Josephus, who wrote towards the end of the first century AD. His treatment of the great religious movement cannot be regarded as completely objective. However, we can be fairly certain of some features of the Essene sect. The Essenes had a kind of monastic settlement near the Dead sea, close to where the shepherds found the scrolls. The Essenes were noted for their piety, their quietism, their renunciation of the worldly ambitions and riches. They lived as a primitive communal sect and held their possessions in common. They could move freely about the country, assured of a welcome in any other lay community in the outskirts of Palestine. There does not seem to be much doubt that the Essene teaching of celibacy, of poverty,

[3] *Universitas, 1966,* Vol. VIII, No. 3, p. 229.

of communal sharing had considerable influence on Jesus.

Authors already committed to certain definite views may shrink from the opinion held in common by the Scrolls and Jesus and early Christianity. In the Scrolls, we find references to crucifixion and some of the teachings of the Sermon on the Mount. Copies of the Old Testament book *Isaiah,* a thousand years older than any previously known Hebrew manuscript of the Old Testament, are known to the Scrolls. There were also Jewish sectarian books which reveal the immediate background of Christianity.

Christianity has much in common with Mithraism. The similarities may be due to direct borrowing or the common Indian background.

The complex ideas of modern science and history seem to have caused a complete inner crisis. The traditional proofs for the existance of God, the ontological argument, the arguments from natural law and design are examined from a new standpoint.

Able, courageous, upright persons find it difficult to accept traditional religion. This is more the product of their intellectual integrity than of wickedness of heart. Traditional views have lost their authority and their psychological justification.

Doubts about the conventional religion are not confined to the relatively few sceptics who had lost their faith, but they seem to have become the common property of a whole generation. The positivist movement represents the scientific reaction against religion.

II

Comte inaugurated the idea of positivism with his law of three stages of cultural development: the first stage of every culture is theological, theology being, for Comte, another name for superstition; the second stage of metaphysics substitutes principles and forces for the ancient gods, and the third stage is positivism which deals with scientific knowledge. The positivist demands that we remain within the bounds of experience. Comte said on April 22, 1851: 'I am convinced that before the year 1860, I shall be preaching positivism in Notre Dame as the only really complete religion.'

According to Logical Positivism nothing can be true or even meaningful, unless it can be understood in terms of sense experience. In ancient Greek thought Protagoras held this view, and Plato criticized it.

Hume holds that there can be no true or meaningful assertions about God, soul and immortality or objective moral standards. He discards beliefs about these as 'sophistry and illusion'. For him only two types of statements had a meaning: (i) statements which are capable of being verified or falsified by empirical observation; (ii) statements of logic and mathematics which are tautologous. Hume observes:

'If we take in our hand any volume of divinity, or school metaphysics, for instance; let us ask, Does it contain any abstract reasoning concerning quantity or number? No. Does it contain any experimental reasoning concerning matter of fact and existence? No. Commit it then to the flames.

For it can contain nothing but sophistry and illusion.'

Professor Ayer asks:

'What is this but a rhetorical version of our own thesis that a sentence which does not express either a formally true proposition or an empirical hypothesis is devoid of literal significance? Logical Positivism believes in formal truths and factual statements whose meaning is guaranteed insofar as they are verifiable or falsifiable by sense experience. He who asserts that there is a God is neither making a false assertion nor making an assertion for which the evidence is inadequate. He is merely uttering a form of words, which is neither verifiable nor falsifiable, is devoid of any significance. Ethical statements are emotive. They arouse feelings. They do not have cognitive reference.'

Kant rejects Hume's view. He holds that we cannot look for the reasons of phenomena from within the world of phenomena. If we get beyond the phenomenal to the noumenal world, we get into a region where the categories of explanation do not apply. In the *Critique of pure Reason*, Kant affirms that the limits of sense experience are the limits of our knowledge about the world. Therefore we cannot have a *science* of metaphysics. To use his own words:

'Metaphysics, a completely isolated and speculative science of reason, which declines all teaching of experience, and rests on concepts only, in which reason, therefore, is meant to be her own pupil, has hitherto not been so fortunate as to enter on the secure path of a science. It cannot be denied, therefore, that the method of metaphysic has hitherto consisted in groping only, and, what is the worst, in groping among mere concepts.'

He denies to processes of thought any access to ultimate truth, which lies beyond the sphere of the phenomenally known. God, freedom and immortality are for him postulates of moral life and not objects of knowledge. Ernest Mach interprets Kant as rejecting any explanation as unscientific, since it goes beyond experience.

To Hume's doctrine of experience, modern Logical Positivists add the technique of linguistic analysis. The Vienna school presents a new logic, which attempts to draw the line between the meaningful and the meaningless, and also exhibits in detail the structure of the meaningful. The apparent meaningfulness of statements about God, soul and immortality are due to linguistic confusion. All forms of metaphysics are discarded as unprofitable enterprises, and religious beliefs are dismissed as nonsense by which we allow ourselves to be deluded. Rudolf Carnap, one of the founder members of the Vienna Circle of Philosophers, wrote in 1930: 'Before the inexorable judgment of the new logic, all philosophy in the old sense, whether it is connected with Plato, Thomas Aquinas, Kant, Schelling or Hegel, or whether it constructs a new "metaphysic of being" or a "philosophy of spirit" proves itself to be not merely materially false, as earlier critics maintained, but logically untenable and therefore meaningless.' Metaphysical vision, theory of life, the justification of a *Weltanschauung* are repudiated. History of philosophy is nothing but an account of the intellectual follies and confusions of mankind. At best, philosophy is a technique for clearing up confusions. It investigates the logical structure of language, and not its content. It is a type of 'secular scholasticism', with a distrust of all categorical certainties.

As a corrective against revelations and mystic gropings, Logical Positivism and Linguistic Analysis have done useful work. The 'truth' experienced by an individual does not give an account of reality. It is not a cognitive state. In the history of humanity, men professed convictions about the superiority of one's own race or class or nation. Convictions, passionately held, though unproveable, have produced holy wars and race conflicts. God, on these views, is not only irrational but cruel, vindictive and uncivilized.

III

On the Positivist view, life ceases to have any meaning or *raison d'être*, and becomes unsupportable. We seem to be trapped in a dungeon, waiting for death and oblivion. If we are not to perish in the void, we have to live by faith. The sense of belonging nowhere, of having no bonds or attachments, has led many people to get back to dogmas, however unintellectual or anti-intellectual they may be. Flight to authority relieves us of the burden of thinking for ourselves. Orthodoxy becomes the refuge of those who wish to believe even the incredible. But in resorting to authority we overlook the moral obligation to think.

Julian the pagan said:

'man should be taught and won over by reason, not by blows, insults and corporal punishments. Those who are in the wrong in matters of supreme importance are objects of pity rather than of hate. We allow none to be dragged to the altars unwillingly.'[1]

The greatest inhibition to religion as spiritual adventure, is the claim of a faith that it offers final solutions.

It would be unfair to deny the great services which religions have rendered to humanity, by preserving the sense of the spiritual, by succouring the sick and the suffering. These are inconsiderable, compared with their claim to absolute authority and the attempt to enforce that claim, by punishment, by torture and even death.

The Vatican newspaper, *L'Osservatore Romano*, in warning Italian Christian democrats against allying themselves with Marxist groups, said:

'The Church has full powers of true jurisdiction over all the faithful and hence has the duty and the right to guide, direct and correct them on the plane of ideas and the plane of action. A Catholic can never prescind the teachings and directives of the Church. In every sector of his activities we must inspire his private and public conduct by the laws, orientation and instructions of the hierarchy.'

[1] Emperor Julian's Edict to the people of Bostia, AD 362.

Such a view is not consistent with freedom of conscience and religious liberty. Religions, by upholding the authority of their organizations, tend to crush the individuality of the people, debase their sense of moral responsibility, and corrupt the conscience of the community.

Doctrine enforced by authority is hostile to human aspiration and growth. We cannot compel belief. The methods adopted by religions to enforce conformity are used by totalitarian systems, which profess to give us absolute certainties. If we shut the doors of the mind and believe that we already possess the truth, we will not find the truth. The dogmatic religions and the totalitarian schemes foster the herd mind and develop the closed mechanistic society. They deify their leaders[1] and make avatars of them. Religious preceptors in our country are sometimes raised to the divine status.

When nationalism becomes itself a religion, and the religious leaders exalt the interests of the nation above those of humanity, religion itself becomes effete. Instead of transcending national limits, religion becomes subordinated to the development of national personality, the fulfilment of the national mission.

[1] A young Russian writer under the pseudonym of Alram Tertz observes: 'Stalin seemed to have been created for the hyperbole that awaited him. Mysterious, all-seeing, omnipotent he was a monument of our age and the only thing he lacked to become God was immortality. Oh, if we had only been clever and ringed his death round with miracles! If we had only declared on the wireless, that he wasn't dead but ascended into heaven, whence he continued to watch us, silent behind his mysterious whiskers! His relics would have cured the paralysed and the possessed, and children at bed time would have prayed at the window, their eyes fixed on the shining stars of the Celestial Kremlin.'

Encounter, January 1960, p. 95.

The nature of man has changed for the worse in recent years, not because he is worse morally or religiously, but because he is ceasing to be an individual. The power, with which a mechanized society endows him collectively, diminishes his individual reality. Most of us are groping, nervous, spiritually disinherited, passionately hungry for we know not what. Unless the mechanized society itself is under spiritual control, the future is full of peril. Man's failure to master the machine is the root cause of his self-division and distress.

There have always been liberal minds, who question the orthodoxies which imprison the human spirit, whether in religion or in politics. Karl Marx revolted against religion on behalf of the humanity of man. The existence of God, according to him, threatens the freedom and dignity of man. Their number has greatly increased with the growth of the scientific spirit. Free and disinterested spirit of inquiry is vital for civilization, and any religion which discourages it has no chance of survival.

IV

The moral abdication of religious leadership has also contributed to the waning influence of religion. Religious leaders are without significant influence in the world, or are themselves secularized by it.

Religion, in theory at least, requires us to renounce the world, the flesh and the devil but in our life the flesh asserts itself, the devil has its due and the world expects us to work in it, making it better or worse. Even religious leaders are worldly in spirit. Even if we are asked to withdraw from life, it is as a preparation for participating in life and reforming it. Humanism is not opposed to religion, and the latter is not incompatible with healthy life. Life is not necessarily spiritual because it is lived primitively, nor are people necessarily fine in character, because they are unfortunate. It is wrong to assume that there is an innate superiority in illiteracy, poverty and disease. Ignorance and poverty are not the attributes of spiritual life. It is true that love, loyalty and courage are found among the rich and the poor. That is no reason why we should acquiesce in poverty.

When we look at the widespread poverty, misery and oppression in large parts of the world, the starving millions in the streets of African and Asian cities, the squalid slums which litter large parts of the world, the tortured inhabitants of Hiroshima and Nagasaki, the concentration camps, massacres of people who yearn for political freedom and race equality, we see how God is abandoned, religion sneered at, love despised and goodness defeated. When we see without blinkers, we realize that our professions are empty, our intentions are hollow. Our religion is only a mask, a pretence, a make-believe. While we preach love and service, often we deny it. When the world is threatened by atomic destruction, when we are piling up nuclear armaments, which is a sure way to annihilation, many of the religious leaders are silent. By condoning the use of nuclear weapons, we are violating the moral principle that evil means must not be used even for attaining ends considered to be good.

We live in a crumbling world without any hope, refuge or light. Our leaders give us advice, so carefully worded that it does not antagonize those in seats of power and authority. They do not set the right example. They fumble and falter in talking about a faith they no longer believe in. In an unbelieving world, faith is proved by action, but the action is so hesitant and infirm. Lenin is reported to have said that if we could show him a dozen Christians who lived their faith as fully as St Paul lived his, then he would become a Christian.

True religion, whether it is of the Hindu sage, of Zarathustra, of the Buddha, of Jesus, of Muhammad, or of Nānak, asks us to meet hatred and violence with calm and dignity. 'Unto him that smiteth thee on one cheek, offer also the other.' Twenty-five million human beings died to bring Hitler down but Hitlerism is not dead. Mass thinking, national pride, race bigotry, lust for power and faith in violence as the supreme arbiter in human affairs—these are not dead. All nations, Communist or non-Communist, seem to have an unshakeable faith in the efficacy of violent action. Even when we come across national disputes or racial persecutions, we find the image of violence trying to solve intractable problems. In the two wars which we saw in our life time, mass murders, diabolical cruelties and deliberate tortures were practised. Religious leaders became crusaders and persuaded honest men and women to believe that they owed loyalty to their own side, however evil it might be. The illusion is spread that we are the good and our enemies are the wicked. The world is divided into criminals and crusaders.[1] Gāndhi insisted on the purity of means as well as of ends. We cannot, as religious men, under any circumstances, justify the immoral and the spiritually degrading means of using hydrogen bombs to gain our ends, however noble they may be. And yet we quote scripture to justify a religion of hate which should be a contradiction in terms.[2] Article 37 of the 39 Articles, for example, states that it is lawful according to the law of God 'to wear weapons and at the command of the magis-

[1] *cf:* Jacques Maritain, referring to the means employed in the Spanish Civil War (including the wholesale killing of the prisoners) and condoned by the Church wrote: 'The problem of the means on which we are for ever insisting is of the greatest importance; it involves all ethics; it is all ethics. It is upon this that Christianity, if it does not wish to abdicate, will be led to affirm in the sharpest way its opposition to the doctrine of force, which holds all means to be good, and which proves this by moving from success to success—in death.' Karl Marx said: 'The idea of God is the keystone of a perverted society. It must be destroyed. The true root of liberty, equality and culture is atheism.' 'Religion is the sigh of the oppressed creature, the heart of a heartless world, just as it is the spirit of a spiritless situation. It is the opium of the people . . . The abolition of religion as the illusory happiness of mankind is required for their real happiness. The demand to give up the illusions about its condition is the demand to give up a situation which needs illusions.' Freud in his *The Future of an Illusion* said: 'When man is freed of religion, he has a better chance to live a normal and wholesome life.'

[2] *cf:* Norman Bentwich: *The Religious Foundations of Internationalism.* 'The Christian religion has more often been a factor for war than for peace. Christian peoples have hated each other for the love of God.' Bismarck defined a pietist as 'a person who tries under the guise of religion to further his own selfish interests'.

Heine described the priest in the verse:

'I know the wise fellows, I know the text,
I know also its author
I know they secretly drank wine
And publicly preached water.'

Thomas Hardy's lines are well known:

'After two thousand years of Mass
we have got as far as poison gas.'

trates, to serve in the wars'. Those who are pleading for disarmament and a warless world will not find this advice sound, which is in marked opposition to the teaching of Jesus in the Gospels. The nuclear tests threaten the existence of a proper environment for the functioning and growth of civilization. We have no right to devastate or even pollute earth, water and air. The philosopher of the French Enlightenment attacked both Church and State. 'Men will never be free,' said Diderot, 'until the last King is strangled with the entrails of the last priest.'

The world is in search of a new morality. There can be only one objective for human endeavour, perfect service and love of fellow men. Philosophy is love of wisdom, and religion should be the wisdom of love, love which redeems suffering man. Religion is lived truth, when the inward and the outward become one.

This is possible only when religion becomes a burning conviction, a consuming fire and not a mere intellectual pastime. The great Catholic theologian, Baron von Hugel, declared that the more orthodox the Christian Catholic became doctrinally, the less sensitive he became morally. Lord Acton wrote:

'The true guide of our conduct is no outward authority, but the voice of God who comes down to dwell in our souls.'

It matters little what we believe, what matters is what we are. Vyāsa, in the *Mahābhārata,* says:

'I have been shouting with raised hands, but nobody listens to me. Through dharma or righteousness, material and artistic developments arise. For what reason do they not adopt it?'[1]

It is the function of religion to turn the world upside down, to make revolutionary demands. If religious men take interest in secular problems, they are convicted of a gross betrayal of religion. Political liberalism and socialist ethics, it is said, are not religion. Theologians are attempting to combine the spirit of religion with secular humanism. Many theologians attempt to come to terms with the contemporary situation and social demands. They are concerned that religion is lacking in personal integrity and social discipline.

V

Besides, religions lack universality of outlook. While they proclaim that all men, whatever be their caste, creed or colour are equal in the sight of God, many religious organizations become intolerant absolutisms, condemning all those who do not accept them to eternal perdition. Religious persecutions, inquisitions, tortures have darkened many pages of the history of religions. Religious bureaucracies are intolerant. In many backward countries, people still believe in spirits, sorcerers and soothsayers.

Religions behave like nation States. Bad citizens belong to it, good neighbours are aliens. The divisions and exclusions, the intolerance and bigotry are violations of normal human relationships. It is bad enough when we have to fight one another for land or food. It is worse when

[1] *ūrdhvabāhur viromy eṣa na ca kaścit chruṇoti me*
dharmād arthaś ca kāmaś ca sa kim artham na sevyate.

we kill one another for doubtful definitions of the unknown. The mysteries of life, instead of binding us with a sense of common destiny, are turning us against one another.

The religious leaders do not tell their followers that the religion they are taught is only one of many, some of them older and perhaps superior in certain respects, and that all its teachings are not beyond criticism. We teach our followers that our religion is logically perfect and spiritually adequate.

The twenty-first Roman Catholic Ecumenical Assembly showed great courage in scanning its own past and admitting the grave wrongs which some of its saintly predecessors had inflicted on humanity. William Makepeace Thackeray wrote: 'The wicked are wicked, no doubt and they go astray, and they fall, and they come by their deserts, but who can tell the mischief which the very virtuous do.' The evil that good men do in the name of their inner illumination and self-righteousness is much greater than what the so called evil men do. Many defenders of faith were offenders against truth. In the name of our religion we have denied brotherhood with men of other faiths, who also 'hunger and thirst' after righteousness.

There are many religious men deprived of beliefs and are wandering, alienated human beings, strangers, men in exile, homeless, isolated, yearning for the voice of the future.

VI

These are some of the difficulties which intelligent men encounter in the matter of religious beliefs. Whatever faith we adopt should be reconcilable with the spirit of science and the ethics of humanism. It should help the growth of the individual and not warp it. It should be in conformity with the growing demands of moral conscience and it should be universalist in spirit. The morally indefensible practices which we adopt in the name of religion have brought disrepute to it, and many thinking people feel that religion is condemned to a slow death. It is on the way out.

We seem to be moving towards a state of no religion. We may sing the old hymns, recite the familiar creeds, pray earnestly for peace on earth, but deep down there is a state of doubt, a mood of uncertainty. In all religions, there is a tendency for radical changes. The Catholic Christians will not be the same again; they are becoming more Protestant. The Protestants feel that there may be a second Reformation.

Every great civilization is an effort to organize, integrate and purify the chaos in men's minds and lead the community forward. Our minds are divided and yet they are receptive and generous.[1] Even if the heavens do not declare the glory of

[1] *cf:* C. G. Jung: 'During the past thirty years, people from all the civilized countries of the earth have consulted me. Many hundreds of patients have passed through my hands, the greater number being Protestants, a lesser number Jews, and not more than five or six believing Catholics. Among all my patients, in the second half of life—that is to say, over thirty-five—there has not been one whose problem in the last resort was not that of finding a religious outlook on life. It is safe to say that every one of them fell ill because he had lost what the living religions of every age have given to their followers, and none of them has been really healed who did not regain his religious outlook. This, of course, has nothing whatever to do with a particular creed or membership of a church.'

The Collected Works, Vol. XI (1958), p. 334.

God, even if they have become an eternal silence of infinite space, even if the world is not a scene of divine purpose but obeys blindly the laws of mechanistic science, men will retain the values which they have inherited from religion within a humanistic framework.

Among all sorrows there is a kind of fraternity. All of us are seekers after truth, rebels who yearn for freedom from the bondage of life to things, objects, abstractions and ideologies. We are in search of the incommunicable secret which binds the dim past, with the disrupted present and the intimidating future.

VII

Nietzsche's statement 'God is dead' is the battle cry of a new movement. Stendhal affirms that the only excuse for God is that he does not exist. There is no need for God either as an explanation for the sun and the stars, or as an answer to man's anxiety. The growth of scientific knowledge of nature and human behaviour, the historical understanding of human progress, and the web of technological culture do not support the hypothesis of any distinctively Divine action. Where was God and what was he doing when bombs were dropped at Hiroshima and Nagasaki? Was he asleep when millions were tortured and murdered in the gas chambers and the concentration camps? Such questions torture men's minds. Man seems to have lost the sense of the sacred. We are engaged in a great human adventure into outer space, when the earth is not yet fit for human habitation.

The theologian, Dietrich Bonhoeffer, wrote about the world that had come of age and stimulated a rejection of the presence of God. He said, 'It is becoming evident that everything gets along without God, and just as well as before. As in the scientific field, so in human affairs generally, what we call "God" is being more and more edged out of life, losing more and more ground.' He wrote from prison:

'Honesty demands that we recognize that we must live in the world, as if there were no God. And this is just what we do recognize—before God! God himself drives us to this realization—God makes us know, that we must live as men who can get along without Him.'[1]

We should get rid of moral and theological irrelevance.

Professor Thomas J. J. Altizer goes further and says:

'Theology itself is coming to confess that ours is a time in which God is dead.

'First we must acknowledge that we are not simply saying that modern man is incapable of believing in God, or that modern culture is an idolatrous flight from the presence of God, or even that we exist in a time in which God has chosen to be silent. . . . A theological statement that proclaims the death of God must mean that God is not present in the world of faith. . . . He is truly absent, he is not simply hidden from view, and therefore he is truly dead.'

[1] *New York Times*, June 6, 1966.

Again:

'Surely it is not possible for any responsible person to think that we can any longer know or experience God in nature, in history, in the economic or political arenas, in the laboratory, or in anything which is genuinely modern whether in thought or in experience. Wherever we turn in experience, we experience the eclipse or the silence of God.'

It is the shape of a world in the throes of death and not breakdown. The world seems to be suffering from neuralgia of the brain, which is madness.

Scepticism, which is said to be the chastity of the intellect,[1] riddles the faith of yesterday and prepares us for the faith of tomorrow. In spite of the total secularization of the world, man will again be able to recapture an understanding of the sacred. We need to find a way back to the living spirit which combines opposites. If the world is to be saved, we must recover the spirit of religion. We are persuaded that we are advancing toward the light; when the darkness is deep, the stars begin to shine. There have been prophetic revolts on behalf of spiritual values in all religions. The seers of the Upaniṣads, Amos, Micah and Isaiah, the Buddha and Jesus leap to our mind. They reformed traditional faiths and made new beginnings. A similar movement is taking place today in men's minds and hearts. We are on the threshold of a new age of spirit.

[1] Santayana.

CHAPTER III

THE QUEST FOR REALITY

I

Philosophy is a wide term including logic, ethics, aesthetics, social philosophy and metaphysics. The last is concerned with the ultimate nature of things. The search for metaphysical certainty has been the source of much that is profound and significant in the history of thought. Metaphysics comprises two main fields. One is ontology derived from the Greek word for being. What is reality, which exists in its own right, and is not dependent on anything else? Metaphysics goes beyond the actual. The other is epistemology, which is derived from the Greek word for knowledge. What can the human mind know with certainty? How does opinion differ from knowledge? What can be known?

II

Archbishop Westcott observed that Greece and India[1] stood for the metaphysical temper, the temper that is not satisfied with the surface of existence, but wishes to know through reflection, whether there is any order, any pattern, any reality behind and beyond the world of existence,

[1] *cf:* the late Professor F. W. Thomas: 'we must, I think, admit, after all, that the Indian man, partly by reason of the antiquity and partly in consonance with the complexity of his social conditions, as well as through deliberate cultivation of reflection, has been more of a thinker than are other men.' *Presidential address* ninth All India Oriental Conference, Trivandrum, 1937.

which gives order and meaning to it. The history of speculative thought has its beginnings in the *Ṛg Veda* and the *Upaniṣads*, with its development in the Jaina and Buddhist thought down till today, is an impressive confirmation of the Archbishop's observation.

Man is said to be a tool-maker. He may also be defined as a pattern-maker. When his cold and hunger are conquered, when his appetites and desires are satisfied, he wishes to know if there is any pattern in things, any meaning in life. Man is afraid of formlessness, irrationality, uncertainty, chaos. He cannot be content with them. 'Joy and anger, sorrow and happiness, worries and fears, come upon us by turns, with ever-changing moods, like music from the hollows, or like mushrooms in the swamp. Day and night they alternate within us, but we cannot tell whence they spring. Alas! Alas! Could we for a moment lay our finger upon their very cause?'[1]

The impulse to philosophy, the ontological disposition, exists in all of us. Has life any meaning, has the world any purpose, does history tend anywhere, do the different parts of the world hang together?

Metaphysics is not an esoteric pursuit. It is a natural propensity, a spiritual necessity of the human mind to seek the presuppositions of thought and existence. It has an important place in the life of every reflecting person, who seeks to understand the cosmos in which he had his being and tries to find a way of life, which gives him a sense of harmony between himself and the world at large. He forms ideas, devises beliefs to

[1] Chuang Tse (335–275 BC).

frame into shape the mass of facts observed. Metaphysics is a reflective attempt to order the whole of our experience. It is a quest for meaning.

III

Some philosophers approach their task from the standpoint of science, others from that of religion, but the greatest use both. Every philosopher is both an analyst and an existentialist. He deals with both facts and values. He is a poet with an intellectual conscience. Analysis without vision is expense of spirit, waste of subtlety. Undisciplined vision, unexamined intuition, sheer passion are the sources of superstition, fanaticism, madness. Philosophical analysis is a corrective to the natural tendency to deceive ourselves with false hopes.

The analytic and the existential tendencies are found in the Upaniṣads and early Buddhism, in Socrates and Plato, in the Middle Ages in the philosophy of the Schools, in Śaṁkara and Spinoza, Bradley and Bergson.

There is always a tension between logical analysis and existential experience. Any adequate philosophy should be sustained by the integrity of reason and the claims of inward experience. In the greatest philosophers, we have both the rigour of logic and the poetry of passion.

Two illustrations may be taken from Western thought, Plato and Kant. Plato's theory of forms is based on logical argument. When he hypostasizes the forms and affirms that absolute beauty and absolute justice are not mere concepts but have their existence in another world, when he subordinates the world of sense to that other world, he is under the influence of the Orphic and the Pythagorean views. What is given does not transcend nature but the aspiration it awakens does.

Plato had a deep sense of alienation and a vision of another world. Death is not the end. There is another world, where the soul has its being before birth and after death. It is not logic or epistemology, that leads to this view, but reflection on man and his conduct. In the *Theaetetus,*[1] Socrates exhorts man to 'become like a God as far as he is able to'. We feel a sense of lack, a privation. We have to grow beyond our present status. Man, as he is, is incomplete.

Kant confined knowledge and science to the world of phenomena. But reflection on the nature of the world led him to the conclusion that it did not constitute the whole of reality, and there were supersensible entities, things in themselves. There were Ideas of reason, of the soul, of the world in its entirety and of God. The realities corresponding to these Ideas could not be construed as objects. They have not a constitutive but only a regulative use. They enable us to organize our experience and estimate its worth. The pursuit of science rests on a faith, a hope and a trust, the faith of reason in its own supremacy or in the rationality of the world.

The examination of our nature as moral agents enables Kant to give a richer and deeper meaning to Ideas. The fact of duty is a positive illustration of the kind of reality to which the ideas of reason point, a reality, which, although having a

[1] p. 176.

definite context, is in no sense an object in the context of experience. For Kant, the contemplation of the starry heaven above should be accompanied by the recognition of the moral law within us.

In Indian thought we have both existentialist distress and rational reflection. The main concern of Indian thought is with the status of man, his ultimate goal. Nature and God are treated as aids to help man to attain security of being, peace of mind. The main interest of Indian thought is practical. Philosophy is a guide to life.

There are many who assume that there would be no unappeased hunger for the unseen in an earthly paradise where poverty and want are abolished and a just society is established. Karl Marx believed that once communism was fully realized and man lived in reasonable and intelligible relation with society, there would be no place for religion in men's minds. Naciketas says in the *Kaṭha Upaniṣad*: 'Man is not to be satisfied with wealth.'[1] We cannot be content with wealth so long as the all-devouring time is in power. We may have all the wealth of the world, and yet we will be unhappy, for man has a desire for eternal life which no political contrivance or economic arrangement can satisfy. There can be no satisfaction in the things that perish.

IV

The metaphysical quest starts with man's dissatisfaction with the actual world. History, astronomical, geological, pre-human and human,

[1] *na vittena tarpaṇīyo manuṣyaḥ.* I.1.27.

appears to be an aimless process of creations and perishings, from which no meaning for the individual human existence seems to be possible. The world seems to be marvellously beautiful, terrifyingly empty. We do not seem to discern any principle in the whole chain of being which demands man's meaningful participation in the adventure of time. The world seems to be a meaningless, vain and futile show. If ultimate nothingness is not all, there should be some meaning behind it all.

Animals are subject to disease, decay and death, but are not capable of distress. Man knows the animals but they do not know him. Some of us behave like animals and our lives are mostly an evasion of ourselves. We should not be content with the satisfactions of immediate desires. The hunger is there for something more than animal satisfactions or even intellectual and aesthetic experiences. *Hitopadeśa* tells us that every morning, on rising, one should think 'which of the great calamities, death, disease or sorrow will happen today?'[1]

Hindu thought looks upon the world as *saṁsāra*, something which flows, which is never steady and abiding. It is a perpetual procession of events where one event supersedes another. The Buddha bases his way of life on the fact of

[1] *uttāyotthāva boddhavyam mahat bhayam upasthitam*
maraṇa-vyādhi-śokānāṁ kim adya nipatiṣyati. I.4.

cf: Bhartṛhari:
ādityasya gatāgataiḥ ahar aha samksīyate jīvitam
vyāpāraiḥ bahu-kārya-bhāra gurubhiḥ kalo na vijnāyate
dṛṣṭvā janma-jarā-vipatti-maraṇam trāsaśca notpadyate
pītva moha-mayīm pramāda-madirām unmatta-bhūtam jagat
Vairāgya-śataka.

suffering, *duhkha*, and asks whether there is a way out of it, out of this existential estrangement of man.

Confucius writes:

> The great mountain must crumble
> The strong beam must break
> And the wise man wither away like a plant.

'Remember, man, that dust thou art and unto dust shall thou return.' Jeremiah cries out:

> 'Cursed be the day when I was born; the day my mother bore me be unblessed. Accursed the man that brought glad tidings to my father, saying "A son was born to you"—and made him glad. That he slew me not from the womb! And that my mother were my grave. Wherefore came I forth out of the womb? To see suffering and grief, that my days are consumed with shame.'[1]

'Man is born to trouble as the sparks fly upward.'[2]

Plato looks upon philosophy as a meditation on death. Christianity built its structure of faith on the foundation of divine despair. St Augustine speaks of 'the ceaseless unrest which marks the temporal life of the individual.'[3]

The consciousness of death is the source of anxiety. If man loses himself in the world and its diversions, his anxiety may be a brief fleeting fear. But man is a thinking being. When he reflects on the finite and limited character of his existence, he is overcome by fear which is, as Heidegger says, 'more primordial than man

[1] XX. 14 ff.

[2] *Job.*

[3] In the *Imitation of Christ* Thomas-a-Kempis writes: 'Thou errest greatly if thou seekest any other thing than to suffer, for all this mortal life is full of miseries and is all beset about and marked with crosses.'

himself.' When the fear becomes conscious of itself, it becomes anguish. The tragedy of the soul is added to the contemplation of the world as mortal. The ability to feel lost is man's tragic destiny and glorious privilege.

V

Modern man feels that he is rootless because he is unaware of his real being. He laments the felt absence of Being, of Reality. He is engrossed by the chances and changes of mere existence. His energy becomes a will to power or a mere striving for security. This is the nihilism which denies absolute value to anything.

But there is a natural Platonism, a horror of absolute chaos, which inclines man to ask if there is any Reality behind the flux. The consciousness of the finiteness and mortality of all our achievements makes us ask, whether there is anything beyond and behind the world process. There is the basic human hunger for a world beyond strife and suffering. If there were not a Beyond, we should have been satisfied with the world process. The suffering individual cries out, in the words of the *Upaniṣad*:

> Lead me from the unreal to the real
> Lead me from darkness to light
> Lead me from death to eternal life

asato mā sad gamaya, tamaso mā jyotir gamaya, mṛtyor mā amṛtam gamaya.

Man can step out of the world and this proves that he is in some sense beyond the world. Man postulates God from a feeling of absolute need.

Faith is confidence in something not seen, not perceived. It is a repudiation of what narrow empiricism reports of the facts, transitory, confused, seemingly unjust. Faith is a postulate, not an ordinary perception. A knowledge of God is naturally present in the heart of man.

In *Genesis*, it is said, if man and woman will only eat the fruit of the one tree, 'ye shall be as God'. The meaning of it is that what we are is not what we should be. In *Leviticus*[1], the Lord demands: 'Ye shall be holy, for I, the Lord your God, am holy.' Christianity affirms that death is not all. The crucified God is not the last word. 'He is risen'. The Easter celebrates triumphantly the resurrection of God. Death has no sting, grave has no victory. Love is the only reality. It is indestructible. All that man can do against it is powerless. Shakespeare knew that time had dominion over all earthly things and it is for man to develop a mood of timelessness, the sense of eternity:

Our revels are now ended, these our actors,
As I foretold you, were all spirits, and
Are melted into air, into thin air;
And, like the baseless fabric of this vision,
The cloud-capp'd towers, the gorgeous palaces,
The solemn temples, the great globe itself,
Yea, all which it inherit, shall dissolve,
And, like this insubstantial pageant faded
Leave not a rack behind, We are such stuff
As dreams are made on; and our little life
Is rounded with a sleep.

In the famous hymn *Abide with me*, Mr H. F. Lyte writes:

[1] XIX.

Change and decay in all around I see
O Thou who changest not, abide with me!

I fear no foe, with Thee at hand to bless,
Ills have no weight, and tears no bitterness,
Where is death's sting? Where, grave, thy victory?
I triumph still, if Thou abide with me.

In Handel's *Messiah* we read: 'Though worms destroy my body, yet in my flesh shall I see God'.

'Heaven's light for ever shines
Earth's shadows fly'[1]

In the *Upaniṣads,* the word *Brahman* refers both to the aspiration in man's soul, the outgrowing of the spirit, prayer as well as the object sought, the Ultimate Reality. The seeking of man is inspired by the Eternal in him. It is the presence of the Infinite that makes him dissatisfied with the finite. Compare the confession in *Romans,* 'we do not know how to pray as we ought, but the spirit himself intercedes for us with sighs too deaf for words.' This view reminds us of the word of God, that Pascal believed he had heard: 'You would not seek me if you had not already found me.'[2] Kafka said, 'one goes abroad to discover the home one has lost.' Gāndhi says:

[1] Shelley.
[2] *cf:* Wordsworth:

Oh! mystery of man, from what a depth
Proceed thy honours, I am lost but see
In simple childhood something of the base
On which thy greatness stands; but this I feel
That from thyself it comes, that thou must give
Else never canst receive.

'I consider it wrong to expect certainties in the world where all else but God, that is Truth is an uncertainty. All that happens about and around us is uncertain, transient. But there is a Supreme Being hidden therein and one would be blessed, if one could catch a glimpse of that certainty, and hitch one's wagon to it. The quest for truth is the *summum bonum* of life.'

Suffering is the result of the conflict in man. He belongs to two worlds, the spiritual and the natural. He is Being and non-being.[1] As a citizen of an earthly state, he is subject to the dominion of death. He also belongs to the world of spirit, not bounded by time.

While Positivism is influenced by the scientific method, Existentialism has for its motive power the religious quest. Existentialism is one of the basic types of thought which appears in the history of philosophy, whenever we stress the difference between the individual being of man and the being of objects in nature. There is a difference between the being of the self and the being of things. Man not only is, but he *knows* that he *is*. His being is open to himself. Knowledge is confined to the world of objects but the self is comprehended from within. There is objective knowledge as well as subjective comprehension. It is sometimes argued that the one thing that is given incontrovertibly is the knowledge of one's own self. We do not know in the same way objects of the world. Existence cannot be deduced from logical principles.

While there are no proofs for the existence of God, there are intimations that the world of our

[1] *sad-asad-ātmaka.*

experience is not self-sufficient. Religious experience is not self-sufficient. Religious experience transcends intellectual, discursive knowledge. Kierkegaard writes in his *Journals*:—

'The majority of men in every generation, even those who, as it is described, devote themselves to thinking, live and die under the impression that life is simply a matter of understanding more and more, and that if it were granted to them to live longer, that life would continue to be one long continuous growth in understanding. How many of them ever experience the maturity of discovering that there comes a critical moment where everything is reversed, after which the point becomes to understand more and more that there is something which cannot be understood. This is Socratic ignorance and that is what the philosophy of our time requires as a corrective.'

Each man shares a world with his fellow-men but he has also a personal world, a world of imaginings, wishes and dreams. The existentialists ask us to start with the immediacy of living experience, which can be grasped existentially from within. They argue that anguish is man's central experience. The world in which we fall in love, commit crimes, utter prayers or lose heart is the most important world of experience.

The Buddha's attitude to abstract, philosophical speculation becomes clear from the sixty-third sermon of the *Majjhima Nikāya,* a part of the *Suttapitaka,* entitled the lesser *Māluṅkya Suttanta.* In it the monk, Māluṅkyaputta, complains that the Buddha has not elucidated certain important questions such as, 'Is the world eternal or not? Is it finite in space or infinite? Are soul and body identical or different? Does the perfected exist after death or not?' The Buddha answers by a parable:—

'Suppose a man were wounded by a poisoned arrow and his friends bring a physician to treat him and suppose the man said, "I will not have the arrow removed or the wound treated until I find out all about the man who shot me, his name, caste, size, personal appearance and residence and also the exact nature of the materials used in making the arrow, the bowstring and the bow," would not such a man die of the poisoned wound, before he found the answers to these futile and irrelevant questions.'

So also the Buddha's Doctrine of the good life does not depend on the nature of the world or the nature of the soul or what will happen to the Buddha after his death. These questions are unprofitable. 'All that I am interested in is the fact of suffering, the cause of suffering, the release from suffering, and the way to the release from suffering.' The Buddha taught a way of life, not a system of thought. His interest was strictly practical, the transformation of man.

Kierkegaard said of his work: 'This is a literary work in which the whole thought is the task of becoming a Christian'. In Jaspers, the emphasis is on becoming a different kind of man. In Jaspers we meet with three different kinds of being, the being of the objective world which is grasped from outside, the being of the self or personal existence which points beyond itself, the being in itself or the transcendent which includes the two other forms of being. Philosophy, for Jaspers, is the striving of the individual to transcend. 'Our enduring task in philosophical endeavour is to become authentic men by becoming aware of being; or, and this is the same thing; to become ourselves by achieving certainty of God.'[1] Heidegger distinguishes between two kinds of life, one authentic and the other unauthentic.

Man is unique in being the one living creature, who is aware of his own existence as something possessing intrinsic significance. He does not treat life as meaningless. Even when he professes a materialist creed which robs existence of meaning or value, he believes as though what he does really matters. He acts on the assumption that the world has meaning or worth. He needs a faith by which to live. The religious instinct cannot be rooted out. If it is not satisfied with a given religion, it seeks another. In all religions, there is faith, a desire to belong, a desire to escape from oneself. There cannot be faith and hope without love. In the political struggle for equality, or the energizing forms of the technological society, in the arts and sciences of the secular world, the principle of love is at work. We love finitude and involvement. These pull us into enjoyment. We suffer and are not at ease. Our mental unhappiness, disease and delinquency are due to the lack of spiritual life. Faith affirms that there is another and better world, a world of super-nature, but faith cannot hold itself apart from reason and experience.

[1] *The Perennial Scope of Philosophy* (1948), p. 159.

CHAPTER IV

FAITH AND REASON

I

The problem of meaninglessness cannot be solved by religious faith alone. The faith has to be sustained by metaphysical knowledge. The worlds of reason and of religion do not turn in different orbits. Indian thought is firm in its conviction that religious propositions should be grounded in reason. The Real is to be known through discrimination, reflection, *vicāra*. The discipline of *manana* prescribed in the Upaniṣads requires us to reflect on what the Scriptures state. *Sāṁkhya* is the name of a system of philosophy which means really investigation.[1] Samkhyā from which Sāmkhya is derived is not always number. It is investigation.[2] Pātañjali uses the term *prasaṁkhyāna* in the sense of supreme knowledge.[3] The intellectual approach to the knowledge of supreme reality is generally insisted on in Indian thought. By discussion is gained illumination of reality.[4] If it does not reach illumination, it is mere weariness of speech.[5] Discussion implies a

[1] Śaṁkara, in his commentary on *Viṣṇu-sahasra-nāma,* quotes from *Vyāsa-Smṛti*: *śuddhātma-tattva-vijñānam sākṁhyam iti abhidhīyate*: *cf*: *Mahabharata*:

> *ñasti vidyā samam cakṣuh*
> *nāsti satya samam tapaḥ.*
>
> (X. 331. 6.)

[2] *Carcā, saṁhyā, vicāraṇā*: *Amara Kośa,* I. 5. 2.

[3] *Yoga Sūtra,* IV. 2. 9.

[4] *vāde vade jāyate tattva-bodhaḥ.*

[5] *vāco viglāpanam hi tat.*

faith that there is truth, and we can approach it through discussion. We have to think out the metaphysical presuppositions and attain personal experience of the religious *a priori*, from which all living faith starts. We need intellectual effort and spiritual apprehension, metaphysics and religion. Only reasoned faith which is most sensitive to doubt and uncertainty can give coherence to life and thought.

Although there are a few Christian theologians like Karl Barth, who protest against the intrusion of reason into the realm of religious faith, who deny the possibility of any philosophy of religion,[1] the main tendency in Catholic and many Protestant forms of Christianity is, however, to use reason for the defence of faith. Religious faith cannot take the place of thinking, but it has to be founded on it. Only through thinking is one able to retain one's faith in religion. Faith has to be sustained by inquiry. Spiritual experience refuses to separate illumination of the mind from purification of the heart.

II

Logical Positivism does not account for the innate quality of man which gives him courage to work in a civilization which is rendered meaningless by it. It makes us forget our debt to the past. We are led to forget our ancestors, even our descendants; even from our contemporaries we are cut off. We are thrown back

[1] Emil Brunner says: 'to deny a "general revelation before that of Christ can appeal neither to Paul nor to the Bible at large" '.

The Letter to the Romans.

on ourselves, and in the end confined to the solitude of our hearts. The systems of the past may not solve our problems or save our souls but they have led us to the present state.

No scientist can get started without the belief that there is a world, that there is order in it and that the human mind is capable of understanding this order. The effort of the scientist to understand a presumably disorderly or incomprehensible world is based on this belief. Without this belief, we will still be feeling that capricious forces manipulate the universe. The change from the age of superstition to that of science is marked by the faith in an orderly universe, intelligible to man. Einstein has a remark inscribed at the hall at Princeton: 'God is very subtle, but he is not malicious'. Every scientist has a vision of the order and unity of the world. He has Job's faith. 'Though he slay me, yet will I trust in him.' These beliefs may be progressively confirmed by experience, but when the scientist starts with them, it is a matter of faith and not an empirically verified truth.

Logical Positivism adopts the verification principle. Any sentence can have factual meaning only if it is capable of verification in sense experience. Religious propositions are not capable of such empirical verification and so do not possess any factual meaning.

The principle of verification is not a self-evident statement; nor is it capable of verification by sense-experience. It is not a statement of the same logical character as those for which it lays down the criterion of meaningfulness. Again, it is not easy to draw the line between meaningful and meaningless statements. Universally accepted scientific principles are not capable of verification by sense experience. We do not deny laws of nature on that account. If we look deeply, we find that the revelation we are said to have in religion is not distinct in kind from that which we have in science. We assume that scientific knowledge is the result of logical deduction and analysis of accumulated data, whereas religious knowledge is one by revelation. Great scientific ideas arise, more or less, like religious revelations. Moses was long troubled by the problem of saving the children of Israel and suddenly had a revelation by the burning bush. Gautama the Buddha enquired for years about the nature of reality and one day sat down quietly under the bo tree when he realized the truth of it all. Archimedes leapt from his bath with a triumphant 'Eureka', having seen in a sudden flash the scientific principle which had long eluded him in his study. After hard work and intellectual commitment to a problem, the scientist suddenly sees the answer by a revelation, as it were. The concepts which modern mathematics and physics use are not directly verifiable in sense experience. They lead to deduction which can be related eventually to experimental situations.

In both religion and science, it is an imaginative leap and not facts that lead to discovery and creation. In science the test is fidelity to the observed data which is the measure of validity of theories. The habit of truth runs deep in the scientist's mind, and it will be always willing to reject established dogma when experience suggests a new truth. Both science and religion promote the sense of human dignity.

Positivism assumes certain answers to the major philosophical problems. It offers a metaphysics of science, a world view which appeals to those who have an enthusiasm for science. Bertrand Russell says: 'The most fundamental of my intellectual beliefs is that the idea that the world is a unity is rubbish. I think that the universe is all spots and jumps, without unity, without continuity, without coherence or orderliness or any of the other properties that governesses love.' This is a statement about metaphysics. Even those who claim that there is no transcendental reality are making metaphysical statements about the nature of the universe. The exclusion of metaphysics is, in the end, the substitution of one form of metaphysics for another.

Even though we may repudiate metaphysical systems from Plato's idealism to Marx's materialism, metaphysical thinking seems to be inescapable. Whenever thought grows conscious of itself there is metaphysics. Even he who denies metaphysics does so as the result of a metaphysics which is not aware of being one.[1] Whenever standards of value are used and criticism is applied, there is metaphysics. The logic of the analytical philosophers is itself based on a

[1] *cf:* H. G. Wells: 'When I was young I thought that all metaphysics were just inflated words, hot air. Then I found that wasn't that simple. It wasn't a case of "take it or leave it. If it doesn't amuse you it doesn't matter". One discovered that one had a metaphysic, a frame of reference, a schema on which you acted whether you knew it or not. The really important thing was whether it was one that worked or one that didn't.'

metaphysics, certain presuppositions about the universe. Whatever value logical analysis has, can be defined only in terms of an attitude to life, which logical analysis by itself cannot establish.

When the Logical Positivists proclaim that experience is the indispensable source of data for philosophical investigation, they protest against abstractions, and appeal to experience. But they limit the word 'experience' to sense experience overlooking the many dimensions which experience has. Even Locke and Hume, who are regarded as the founders of modern empiricism, admit the existence of two kinds of experience, one from sensation and the other from reflection or introspection. We have moral, aesthetic and religious experience also. The experience of the one of Plotinus is a spiritual experience. Our intense experiences, the passion for knowledge, the excitement of beauty, the power of goodness, the sense of the numinous cannot be excluded from the world of empiricism.

Experience is not exclusively what comes through science and scientific method. The dissociation of intellect from the other sides of human life is the prominent feature of Logical Positivism. When we speak of sciences, we include under the term not only mathematics, physics and biological sciences but also social sciences and those which deal with spiritual values.[1] Any serious attempt at philosophical

[1] Professor C. D. Broad of Cambridge says in the Preface to his *Five Types of Ethical Theory*: 'It is perhaps fair to warn the reader that my range of experience, both practical and emotional, is rather exceptionally narrow even for a don. Fellows of colleges, in Cambridge, at any rate, have few temptations to heroic virtue or spectacular vice;

interpretation will have to consider all data of experience.

Science does not claim to deduce a moral code from the observation of natural phenomena. No scientific analysis can prove that he who bears false witness is doing something wrong, or that it is better to suffer wrong than to do wrong, or that it is better to die than to kneel down to the powers of the world. This sense of obligation cannot be explained as the result of the necessities of social survival. The dignity of man who chooses to oppose the society that surrounds him points to the working of a principle superior to society. The sense of moral obligation is difficult to explain in terms of natural science. Ludwig Wittgenstein says: 'Even if every possible scientific question were answered, the problems of our living would still not have been touched at all.'

Metaphysical theories are human constructions, interpretations of the nature of the world, and are tested by their adequacy to the observed data, by their capacity to coordinate positive knowledge. They are not mere speculations but interpretations of experience. In the case of

---

and I could wish that the rest of mankind were as fortunately situated. Moreover, I find it difficult to excite myself very much over right and wrong in practice. I have, *e.g.* no clear idea of what people have in mind when they say that they labour under sense of sin; yet I do not doubt that, in some cases, this is a genuine experience, which seems vitally important to those who have it, and may really be of profound ethical and metaphysical significance. I realise that these practical and emotional limitations may make me blind to certain important aspects of moral experience. Still, people who feel very strongly about any subject are liable to overestimate its importance in the scheme of things. A healthy appetite for righteousness, kept in due control by good manners, is an excellent thing, but to "hunger and thirst after" it is often merely a symptom of spiritual diabetes.'

scientific theories, what we can verify is their consequences, insofar as these can be calculated and observed. We do not observe electrical energy, gravitation or relativity but we calculate what will be observed, in carefully determined circumstances, if these are true, and then verify whether they are actually observed or not. This is indirect verification. Metaphysical theories are capable of such indirect verification. F. H. Bradley says: 'what may be, if it must be, it is'. Logically necessity is the clue to the nature of reality.

Scientific theories are not transcripts of reality. They are ways of ordering our experience of reality. In our knowledge of the physical world there is our experience on the one side and the theory which is our creation on the other. The appeal of metaphysics is to a judgment more basic than either sense experience or rational logic. It attempts to assess the reasons for and the limitations implicit in the presuppositions of science and logic.

The kind of proof is not different in science from that in religion. Where we cannot prove, we believe. This element of faith is inevitable in any field of thought. Without the adoption of a working hypothesis, our mind is helpless and dumb. We devise experiments to test the validity of working hypotheses. Religious ideas are also tested and judged by the lives and experiences of those who adopt them. There is an essential similarity of purpose in seeking truth. Science and religion need not be in warring camps or separate watertight compartments. The conflict is derived largely from ignorance of each other, from misunderstanding the methods of science and failure to appreciate the deepest insights of religion. Mutual appreciation is growing and we are slowly realizing that religious truth is profoundly scientific.

There are metaphysicians who claim that they are also empiricists insofar as they deal with being *qua* being. They all start with the basic datum that something exists.

All the same, Positivism helps to release the nature and purpose of religion from magic, superstition and folklore with which it got confused. While it liberates us from religious obscurantism, it should not become a scientific obscurantism which distorts science itself by imposing on it wrong ideas of exactitude and verification.

III

If the heavens declare the glory of God, nature is the mediator. We reach the unmediated by the mediated. The basic fact that there is a world at all, that something exists with its qualities and relations calls for inquiry. How does it happen that there is something rather than nothing? Parmenides raised the question 'Why is there not nothing?' Being is already there without reason or justification. It is not exhausted by any or all of its manifestations, though it is there in each one of its manifestations. The world with its order, design and evidence of purpose cannot be traced to non-intelligent matter. The world order, beauty, movement and contingency form part of the proof of God and militate against any kind of materialism. Through the discovery of the intelligible world we reach truth.

Materialism is the theory which regards all the facts of the universe as explicable in terms of matter and motion. Biological phenomena are reduced to physio-chemical terms. Neurologists hold that all mental processes are explicable in terms of physics and chemistry. They know that there is a difference between consciousness and unconsciousness and since they cannot account for it in terms of science, they deny its existence. Consciousness is an unnecessary hypothesis. It is not a datum that is observable. It is argued that we use the concept of consciousness though there is no such thing.[1]

We do not regard consciousness as an object but it is that which enables us to observe objects. It is the name for the observing. It is not an object or quality of an object. If there is observing or thinking, there must be an observer or thinker.

We have had in India, as in Greece, systems of materialism. They hold that this world and other worlds have come to exist by the chance collision of innumerable atoms, moving with immense velocity through the void. Matter thinks. There is no God. There is no future life for man. Death is a ceasing to be. Whatever exists is material. Sense perception is the basis of knowledge. That which is desirable in life is pleasure and it is not beyond man's reach. There is no

[1] Professor J. Z. Young in his Reith Lectures on *Doubt and Certainty in Science* dismisses consciousness altogether, because, if consciousness 'is a thing in the ordinary sense, it could be observed directly like any other object'. Since it cannot be observed, he concludes that it must be rejected as an 'occult quality'.

other world and death is the end of all.[1] It is difficult on the materialist hypothesis to account for the emergence and progressive advance of man with moral and spiritual qualities.

Dialectical materialism is suggested as an improvement on naturalistic materialism. In this view, matter is said to be not inert but auto-dynamic. For this theory, Marx is indebted to Hegel. Dialectic, for Hegel, is the advance of thought effected by overcoming contradictory or opposing theories. By this process we discover a wider synthesis which comprehends and reconciles the contradictions formulated in the thesis and the antithesis. In dialectical materialism, the opposition of forces in nature takes the place of logical contradiction. The process of development in nature is one in which a series of insignificant quantitative changes lead to abrupt or sudden qualitative changes. Imperceptible changes of temperature result in the change of water into ice or steam. If development of nature is a struggle of opposites, social revolutions express class struggles. 'Revolutions made by oppressed classes are quite natural and inevitable phenomena.' Though social ideas are the product of the material conditions of life, they also react on the material conditions. Marx says, 'Theory becomes a material force as soon as it has gripped the masses.' It is the business of the revolutionaries to spread theories and translate them into action.

We cannot equate logical contradictions with opposing forces in nature. From the way in which phenomena occur in nature, we cannot

[1] *See* Radhakrishnan: *Indian Philosophy*, Vol. I, Ch. V.

deduce how human beings should behave. Dialectic is possible with thought and not with matter.

IV

All metaphysicians, who attempt to account for the facts of experience, do not adopt physicalism as the ultimate truth. A scientific approach does not necessarily lead to materialism. Besides, our knowledge of this world is limited. The beginning and the end are not known. The middle part which is in flux is what we know. A comprehensive knowledge of the world is difficult to acquire. Man does not know the totality of the universe. Again, scientific observation tells us that a plant requires sunlight for its growth, but observation does not tell us why it requires sunlight. Descriptions give us observable features of things and events. Explanations attempt to account for the observed data. They seek to determine the laws according to which events occur. In what is called scientific method, which is one of the most powerful instruments devised by the human mind, we have both direct observations and explanatory theories or interpretations. Despite all the results of scientific research, life remains a mystery. Our true realization of the world is brought about by exposing ourselves to the all-pervading mystery of existence. There are two different realms of knowledge: the realm of facts and the realm of values. Besides knowledge, we have appreciation and reverence. These are gifts of intuitive understanding by a man's whole consciousness. It is a total response to reality.

Metaphysical truth involves the exercise of intuitive understanding.

Scientific metaphysicians like Lloyd Morgan, Bergson, Alexander and Whitehead claim that they start with experience and their theories are meant to account for the facts observed. They hold that there is an empirical route to metaphysical reality. They are empirical metaphysicians. They not only describe facts but attempt to account for them. It is a never-ending attempt to clarify the mysterious. Luck or chance is no explanation.

The *Taittirīya Upaniṣad*[1] distinguishes matter, life, mind, intelligence and spirit in the world process. In the world, to use Leibniz's words: 'there is nothing fallow, nothing sterile, nothing dead'. There are no sharp cleavages. The gradation from one order of being to another is so imperceptible, that it is impossible to draw the line that shall distinctly mark the boundaries of each. Everything in nature is linked together. All beings are connected together by a chain of which we perceive some parts as continuous while others escape our attention. Light and darkness are two distinct entities but we do not know when one passes into the other.

For the Chinese, nature or the Tao is the all-embracing mystery. It is the sudden force that orders the entire universe. It is nameless though the source of all life and existence. 'Before heaven and earth were produced, there was that which was formless, yet complete . . . Its real name we know not; we call it the way that we may be

[1] *See* Radhakrishnan: *The Principal Upaniṣads*, p. 526 ff.

able to express it.'[1] The Tao contains within itself the male and the female principles, the Yin and the Yang. If we equate Tao with nature, the early Chinese philosophers affirm that there is a transcendental side to nature, *Heaven*, *Tien*. We cannot penetrate the ultimate mystery. 'The true sage does not try to know Heaven.'[2] We can live it, but we cannot know it. The Chinese thinkers were greatly impressed by the majesty and the mystery of nature.

The universe began its history in a state of relative simplicity. It has grown increasingly larger with the lapse of ages. Lloyd Morgan adopts the theory of emergence. In certain cases, when elements of a complex are organized in a certain pattern, a new synthesis is derived which shows a quality that could not have been predicted from the knowledge of the constituent elements, before they were so organized. This quality is genuinely new, but it is not an additional factor which might be isolated, alongside the other elements in the complex. It results from the total organized pattern.

When Alexander speaks of mind as an emergent quality, he means that, in one sense, it is identical with an organized structure of neural processes. There is no purely mental factor over and above these. Certain organizations of neural processes manifest a completely new quality, conscious awareness. While it is related to the properties of its neuro-physiological base, it has to be explained in terms of its own characteris-

[1] *Tao Te Ching*, I. 25.

[2] Hsun Ching (3rd Century BC) quoted in E. R. Hughes *Chinese Philosophy in Classical Times* (1942), p. 228.

tic ways of functioning. For Alexander, mind is not the highest possible emergent quality. The religious sentiment of aspiration, the feeling that we are 'moving about in worlds not realized' suggest that there may be a higher quality beyond mind. This, Alexander calls deity. Deity is 'the next highest emergent quality', which the universe is engaged in bringing to birth. The universe is producing beings who are bearers of deity as we are bearers of mind. Its aim is to produce godlike beings. The cosmic process is a value-making one.

Alexander speaks of God as the whole infinite universe, in which matter, life and mind have emerged and which is pregnant with the still higher quality of deity. In this sense, God is the whole universe as tending towards this new quality. The religious sentiment witnesses empirically to our feeling that we are caught in this movement and to 'the sustainment which the universe in its tendency towards deity gives to our mind'. Alexander calls this movement the *nisus* of space-time. We note the presence of this *nisus*, this upward thrust. The world is a creative process where different levels emerge at different stages. To account for this creativity, for the stupendous labour of evolution, space and time are not enough. They cannot account for organized systems bearing new qualities at their distinctive levels. Alexander admits this when he speaks of a *nisus* or a creative tendency. Temporal succession is not creative advance. The impressive fact is that nature has produced a sequence of organized structures in which new levels of organization release new qualities and new powers of functioning. This whole process deepens the mystery of creation.

While Descartes holds that the existence of God is logically demonstrable, Pascal adopts the concept of a hidden God who reveals himself in the exceptional and the miraculous and not in the regular course of nature. We have either a God of revelation or a godless world. The God who reveals himself to certain chosen people, who makes himself known to each person as he wills, is a God who breaks in upon a world which would otherwise seem to lack his presence.

Some theologians point to gaps in our knowledge of nature and hold them to be the sphere where the special creative activity of God operates. This is a dangerous procedure for, as our knowledge increases, the gaps diminish and little scope is left for divine activity and God is edged out. It is misleading to answer difficult problems of nature and history by saying that they show the hand of God. We cannot have two different realms, one where blind soulless nature functions and another where God's creative activity interferes capriciously and ties up loose ends. The universe is not a dead expanse into which God breathes life on suitable occasions. It is man in the making. The development from a primaeval nebula to modern man is without any sudden break in continuity. Man is nature's supreme masterpiece. The great creative process which is already implicit in the simplest particles of matter reaches a crucial stage in man. The best is yet to be and man has still a great deal to learn. Man knows the process of evolution and works consciously for its furtherance. The long process of evolution, the terrestrial formation, the emergence of life, the struggle of mind to rise out of its insentience, the growth of intellect and the intimations of something larger than intellect are not the result of chance. Modern scientists declare that the cosmic process is a steady unfolding from matter to man. Out of the mass of energy at the beginning, we have first the genesis of atoms and molecules. When cooling set in, many creatures, plant and animal and through successive mutations man, arose. There is a structural law of the universe, a fundamental principle of nature. We feel that matter possesses a tendency to organize itself in more and more complex arrangements. No stream rises higher than its source. 'In my end is my beginning.' Intelligent, purposeful beings could not have evolved in a mindless universe.[1]

Behind the development of this universe, there is the Reality of a being, consciousness, bliss, *sat, cit* and *ānanda*. It is the self of all things, one and eternal. All beings are united in that self but divided by a separatist consciousness. Whatever is or seems to be is a variation of being which contains all there is or may be and yet is something purer and more ultimate and essential than any particular vanishing thing. 'Why callest thou me good? There is none good but one, that is, God.' Every manifestation is imperfect because it is a manifestation. Existence is standing out, *ex-sistere*. It stands out from unity of Being. It is on the plane of manifestation. Everything manifested is involved in relativity. Māyā is the objectifying or manifesting

[1] The writings of Teilhard de Chardin confirm this view.

tendency. If the power of manifestation were excluded from the nature of the Absolute, it would not be the Absolute.[1] The empirical variety, the world of existence has its roots in the Absolute. The Divine is in the relative though not fully in it. We are diverse and yet near by the degree of our participation.

Natural Theology gives an explanation of the world in terms of theism. Spinoza says: 'The more man understands individual objects the more he understands God.' The world must have been planned and brought into being by an active intelligent spirit. The late Dr F. R. Tennant mentions five sets of facts as offering a basis for a teleological argument for theism: (i) the adaptation of human thought processes to the objects with which they are concerned, (ii) the adaptation of parts to whole in each living organism, (iii) the adaptation of the inorganic part of nature to the production, maintenance and development of living organisms, (iv) the beauty and sublimity of nature and (v) the facts of moral obligation, social values, etc. There are valid objections to these arguments. From a small fragment of the contemporary world, we cannot argue to the whole. The world and its history as a whole are unique and so the argument does not hold. Besides, we argue, by analogy, from our embodied selves and their operations within the world to a mind which is unembodied and its operation in the world as a whole.

[1] *cf:* Angelus Silesius:

'I know that without me
God can no moment live
Were I to die, then he
No longer could survive.'

Empirical science does not give us knowledge of God. It does not prove God's existence and attributes. And yet we feel that this cosmic process is inspired by a supreme Reality. The world is not only a manifestation of God's being but also a veil behind which he is eternally concealed. The world as we know it is the manifestation of a deeper reality which is beyond human comprehension. Our attitude in this matter is best expressed by what Plato puts into the mouth of Simmias in *Phaedo*:

'I think Socrates, as perhaps you do yourself, that about such matters it is either impossible or supremely difficult to acquire clear knowledge in our present life. Yet it is cowardly not to test in every way what we are told about them, or to give up before we are worn out with studying them from every point of view. For we ought to do one of the following things; either we should learn the truth about them from others; or we should find it out for ourselves; or, if this is impossible, we should take what is at least the best human account of them, the one hardest to disprove, the sailing on it, as on a raft, we should voyage through life in the face of risks—unless one might be able by some stouter vessel, some divine account, to make the journey with more assurance and with fewer perils.'

Kepler closed the last volume of his work *De harmonia mundi* with these words:

'I thank Thee, O Lord our creator, that Thou hast let me see the beauty in Thy work of creation and in the works of Thy hands, I rejoice. See, I have here completed the task to which I felt called. I have made the most of the talent Thou hast given me. I have proclaimed the splendour of Thy works to the men who will read these arguments, as far as I with my imperfect mind have been able to grasp them.'

Einstein, the greatest scientist of our age, said:

'The cosmic religious experience is the strongest and noblest mainspring of scientific research. My religion consists of a humble admiration of illimitable superior spirit, who reveals Himself in the slight details we are able to perceive with our frail and feeble minds. That deeply emotional conviction of the presence of a superior reasoning power, which is revealed in the incomprehensible universe, forms my idea of God.'[1]

V

The problem of evil has always been regarded as a serious obstacle to belief in the Supreme. Hume's statement puts the case thus: 'Is he (God) willing to prevent evil, but unable? Then he is impotent. Is he able but not willing? Then he is malevolent. Is he both willing and able? Then whence is evil?' The problem of evil and suffering tends to destroy faith in God. How can we defend the justice and righteousness of God in the face of the fact of evil, moral and natural, acts of God and sins of human nature, everything from earthquakes and cancer to humanity's long record of betrayal and corruption? We live

[1] *The Universe and Dr. Einstein* by Lincoln Barnett, p. 95.

so close to the possibility of the extinction of humanity, that we cannot believe in a God who controls our destinies.

According to *Genesis*, God created the world perfectly good and its first inhabitants in the Garden of Eden were innocent and without blemish. It was the serpent which introduced evil into the world. But the existence of the evil serpent is incompatible with an infinitely good and powerful God. We cannot dismiss evil as unreal, if not illusory. Christian theology developed the theory of the fall of man. It was accepted by St Augustine, though it was questioned by heretics like the Albigenses. Calvin holds that 'all are not created in equal condition; rather eternal life is foredoomed for some, eternal damnation for others'. This view was adopted by the medieval Christian schools. Newman calls original sin the 'aboriginal calamity'.

Is God the Creator of evil or is there another power equal and parallel to God? Is manichaen dualism the truth? Manichaen dualism holds that this world was created not by God but by the Prince of Evil. Physical matter is incurably corrupt though each one of us has a particle of divine light imprisoned in him. The forces of light do not have an ultimate guarantee of victory; evil might in the long run prove triumphant. This kind of dualism gives us a God who is finite and limited and not all-powerful.

That evil and suffering exist is certain. We cannot dismiss them as merely negative. We have a great deal of useless suffering, hopeless sorrow.

The highest kind of value can only reside in beings who are capable of making deliberate choices and are morally responsible for the choices which they make. Such moral responsibility is impossible if we are not free to choose between alternatives, some of which are less good or more evil than others. If human beings are to be capable of the highest kind of value, we should allow for their making wrong choices. It is up to us to make right choices.

The world is not like a mechanical assemblage of independent parts; it is like an organic system animated by a principle of growth. Over the centuries, an all embracing plan is unfolding itself. The world is moving to the manifestation of free spirits into whom the souls of men are evolving.

Some existentialists affirm that man is blessed or cursed with the freedom of choice. The human being alone among others can choose from a variety of possibilities. When man is truly human, he accepts this freedom and overcomes the anxiety and despair by committing himself to a way of life. If this way of life is spiritual, his despair is overcome.

According to this view, evil is an evolutionary by-product resulting from resistance to the spiritual ascent inherent in matter. It is not the result of the fall of man but his rise, gradual ascent. There is suffering because the world is not perfect but is in a state of growth. Human effort has a value, which is enhanced by suffering. The world has to fight the internal hazards of its own growth. Many individuals may be cut short in their upward flight. For the success of this effort, pain and suffering become necessary. Nothing is inevitable in the growth of the world.

The world process is a continuous search, a continuous effort. The world grows through failures. Pain is the price we pay for the growth. Suffering conceals the power to grow. The suffering of the saints is creative and leads us upward to the kingdom of spirit, the universal advance for which the world is intended. Human life entails evil. The existence of good human beings implies the existence of bad human beings and that means the existence of evil and suffering. If there were no suffering, no evil, no imperfection, there would be no purpose in human action. All life is a struggle against pain and evil and without the latter, there would be no life. The motive for every action is the desire to avoid pain and evil.

As for physical evil, the world could not have been a training place for the development of moral character, unless men's bodies and their environments had consisted of objects with fixed properties and subject to general laws. If the bodies and the environment of sentient beings were of this character, they would sometimes occasion suffering to innocent persons and animals. Such suffering is not willed by God either as an end or as a means. It is tolerated by him as an inevitable collateral consequence of the only condition under which free agents can develop moral qualities and exercise choice. The world is not a pleasure garden, it is a moral gymnasium.

The whole problem assumes the anthropomorphic view of God. If God is a living person, he must also have evil in him. All this is relevant only if God is treated as a human person. We come to repudiate anthropomorphism and look upon the Divine as light too wondrous for human words, too blinding for human eyes. Dionysius, the Areopazite, affirms, in the spirit of Hindu and Buddhist thought, 'God does not belong to the category of existence or to that of non-existence.'

VI

The world has grown from a state of mere materiality to one of life, from life to animal consciousness, from animal consciousness to human intelligence. It now must progress from the level of human intelligence to that of spirituality. For cosmic evolution has not come to a stop with the advent of intelligence. There must still be an evolution in man's psychical nature. The psyche of the individual must expand. The purpose of religion is to help us advance from this world of divided consciousness, with its discords, dualities, to a world of harmony, freedom and love.

In India we say that we must transform our nature, grow from the slavish, unregenerate condition of ignorance to a state of wisdom. This is the religious quest. From the disruption of being we must rise to the articulation of being. The Buddha echoed these words, and so did Ezekiel: 'Thus said the Lord God—I will put a new spirit within you; and I will take the stony heart out of their flesh and will give them a heart of flesh.' According to *Proverbs*, 'the spirit of man is the candle of the Lord'.

Orpheus believed that the soul was 'the son of the starry heaven', that its natural aim was to transcend this earthly life. Similarly, Plato in the *Allegory of the Cave* reveals that most men accept as reality the shadows cast from a light they do not see. A philosopher who leaves the cave may see the light, the Absolute. He then must return to the cave and explain what reality actually is, though the chances are that he will be considered insane. So it is with seers. In time, however, the philosopher will educate other men to the love of wisdom, which is the fine flower of serenity.

Jesus says that unless we are reborn, suffer a change of consciousness, *metanoia*, we will not be saved. In the Fourth Gospel, Jesus says, 'I am the Truth'. We are called upon to follow the example of Jesus. We are to be made like unto him, by bringing our natural desires and expectations unto subjection to the Universal purpose. According to William Law, 'To have salvation from Christ is nothing else but to be made like unto him; it is to have his humility and meekness, his love of God, his desire of doing God's will'. Jesus asks us to free ourselves from priestly control and to undergo spiritual growth. We must be born again, born of the spirit of Truth. And so a twelfth-century Sufi mystic, Ayn Al-qudat at Hamadhani: 'He who is born from the womb sees only this world; only he who is born out of himself sees the other world.'

The world is not a static mechanism. It is a process. Man is evolving into a higher species. He has to realize new possibilities. The process of man's evolution is unfinished; it is to be completed. The inexhaustibility of the source of the universe is the ground of our assurance that it will continue to grow in future till the Kingdom of Spirit is attained. The future of man should be conceived to be, if we use our freedom rightly, a gradual ascent to divine perfection. The cosmic process will not have finished its long journey until every soul has entered into the blissful realization of its own divinity. To achieve a Kingdom of God on earth is the passion of the universe.

Happiness is not the end of life. A life-time of happiness would be utter boredom. Growth to fulfilment is the end. We are in this world not to be happy but to grow. All growth includes moments of struggle and pain.

'Growth' is a key word here. An ethical personality is not something with which we are born, it is not something given to us. Each of us is a welter of differing and often conflicting impulses and potentialities. We deplete so much of our powers in life because of the way in which this desire cancels out that one, this impulse is countered by another. We invent as we go on, we create ourselves out of our follies and contradictions. We have the dark urges of our own blood to tantalize us with impossible satisfactions endlessly withheld. If to be a person is to have potentialities, then we must be ever mindful of the fact that these are potentialities for evil as well as for good. What we have to do is to create ever more ethical personalities in the course of living. We do so if, instead of trying to feed on the lives of others, to live on them and off them, we are devoted to enhancing the lives of others.

The Hellenistic fathers hold that man is not

created by God in a perfect condition, fulfilling the divine intention at the human level of existence. Man is still in the process of creation. God's purpose for man is steadily worked out. He slowly brings men into their glory or perfection. Men in deepest need, victims of estrangement find themselves blessed by the gift of grace. They may not know whence the grace comes but it is an intimation of a presence that transcends our closed systems of thought.

We cannot account for this cosmic process if we do not assume the Divine Reality which sustains and inspires the process. Such a belief is the source of life, meaning and beauty. We start with the world and get to the Spirit. The world has value and goodness. We live by that faith and surrender to death overcoming all doubts and discords. The world is the beginning of the cosmic process and not the end of it. The world is the place where human souls grow into spirits.

CHAPTER V

RELIGION AS EXPERIENCE OF REALITY

I

Indian thought believes in the reality of spiritual experience. Experience is the fruit of knowledge.[1] Knowledge should lead to realization. We move to another intensity, a deeper communion. All thinking which goes deep enough ends in experience. Experience achieves clarity concerning itself through thought. By theoretical knowledge we cannot attain fulfilment. *Theoria* or contemplation is the Greek word which denotes experience of the eternal.[2]

When God revealed himself to Job, the latter said in awe: 'I have heard of Thee by the hearing of the ear, but now mine eye seeth Thee.'[3] 'Blessed are the pure in heart for they shall see God.' All life is an encounter and the supreme encounter is of man with God, what is called in the colophon of the *Bhagavadgītā*, '*kṛṣṇārjuna-saṁvāda*'. Man cannot know God, unless he comes into contact with him in a personal encounter as an object of worship. In Chapter XI of the *Bhagavadgītā*, which is a magnificent outpouring of noble poetry, Arjuna sees God as the entire universe. Arjuna is blinded by the dazzling brilliance. The veil is rent. The Divine bursts the

[1] *anubhavāvasānam eva vidyāphalam vigñāya prajñām kurvita.*

[2] *pustake likhitā vidyā yena sundarī japyate*
siddhir na jāyate tasya kalpakotiśatair api. Ṣaṭkarmadīpikā.

[3] *Job*, XLII. 5.

limits of space, cracks the very bounds of existence. The Divine fills the sky, the universe, space. The world coursed through Him like a cataract. The spirit of this vision is remarkably close to what the Jewish, Christian and Muslim seers have testified about their own experiences.

As Augustine and his mother talked together of the life in heaven, as they contemplated the notion of eternity, they stretched beyond themselves and touched for a moment, in a supreme effort of the heart, the very limits of beatitude. If the obstructions of the world are silenced and the momentary exaltation is sustained, they would have entered into heaven. Augustine says:

'So we said: if to any man the tumult of the flesh were to grow silent, silent the images of earth and water and air, and the poles of heaven were silent also; if the soul herself were to be silent and, by not thinking of self, were to transcend self; if all dreams and imagined revelations were silent, and every tongue, every sign . . . were to become hushed, and He Himself alone were to speak . . . without them; just as, a moment ago, we two had, as it were, gone beyond ourselves, and in a flash of thought had made contact with that eternal wisdom, which abides above all things—supposing that this state were to continue, that all other visions, visions of so different a kind, were to be withdrawn, leaving only this one to ravish and absorb and wrap the beholder in inward joys . . . —would not this be "Enter into Thy Master's joy"? And when shall that be? Shall it be when "we shall

all rise again", though we "shall not all be changed".'[1]

Zen Buddhism distrusts logical analysis. We must know with all our being and not with any part thereof. Existentialists contend that all truth is subjective. It is to be felt from within and not acquired from without. Freedom can be attained here and now. *Mokṣa* (spiritual freedom) is not in a particular place, nor has one to go to some other village to obtain it; the destruction of ignorance, which is the knot of the heart, and is known as *mokṣa*.[2]

The true form of the Reality should be known through one's own clear eye of understanding (*bodhacakṣu*) and not through (the proxy of) a scholar; the true form of the (full) moon should be known by means of one's own eyes only; how can it be known by proxy?[3] The *guru* or preceptor is one who removes the blinkers from the eyes and helps us to see.[4] *Viveka-cuḍāmaṇi* observes that the experience should be one's own and not a mere echo of what another has felt. Experience is direct, unmediated. It is knowledge by acquaintance. It is characterized by our feeling of absolute certainty. When we feel the sunshine we do not doubt its reality.

[1] Rex Warner's E.T. of the *Confessions of Saint Augustine.*

[2] *mokṣasya na hi vāso'sti na grāmāntaram vā*
ajñāna-hṛdaya-granthi-nāśo mokṣa iti smṛtaḥ.

Śiva-Gītā (XIII. 32.

[3] *vastusvarūpaṁ sphuṭabodha-cakṣuṣā*
svenaiva vedyaṁ na tu paṇḍitena
candra-svarūpaṁ nija-cakṣuṣaiva
jñātavyam anyair avagamyate kim.

Viveka-cūḍāmaṇi: 54.

[4] *ajnāna-timirāndhasya jñānānjana śalākayā*
cakṣur unmīlitāṃ yena tasmai sri gurave namaḥ.

Even as we admit a mystery behind the cosmic process, we recognize a mystery behind the flux of mental states. All cognition implies a subject that is conscious of itself and is identical with itself throughout the diversity of its cognitions. It is a self that *has* and not *is* its experiences. It is something over and above these experiences.[1] The self has a body but is not the body; it has an emotional life but is not a set of emotions. It has an intellect but is not the intellect. These are instruments of experience, of perception and action. As instruments of experience, they are changeable and impermanent. They can be disciplined and deliberately used. The self is not a set of perceptions, emotions and thoughts. It is pure self-consciousness. The self is distinct from the states in which it manifests itself and is identical with itself throughout its manifestations.

One cannot doubt the existence of the self of which one is conscious. It is an identity of spiritual being. Kant tells us that the subject or self has its reality beyond the space-time world of phenomena. While we can know in self-knowledge *that* it is, we cannot know *what* it is —knowledge of the character. The *what* of the self gained through introspection is not, for Kant, discernment of the nature of the self as *subject*, but only of the self as an object which is a mere appearance in time of the timeless real self. Kant refers to man's two-fold nature. As belonging to the phenomenal or the sensible world, he is determined, as belonging to the noumenal or the

[1] *yeṣu vyāvartamāneṣu yad anuvartate tat tebhyo bhinnam.*
Vacaspati in *Bhāmatī*.

super-sensible world, he is free. 'Greater is he that is in you than he that is in the world.' Man is free to disobey the law of morality. The inexplicable duality of the human spirit is due to the function of the spirit in him which behaviourism in psychology and determinism in sociology overlook. Each individual should mature into a seeing human being. The Buddha asks us to be awakened.

Insight into reality, though inaccessible to reason, is consistent with it. It reflects back on the rational, completing it and endowing it with significance; that which transcends the rational need not violate it. There is a higher logic of spirit which comprehends but does not annul the rational. Though truth cannot be tied in words, through paradox and poetry it is suggested. It is indicated but not described. In art problems are solved not by concepts but by shapes and symbols. While the labour of thinking is never finished, the creations of art are complete. The poet says the unsayable in the language of symbols. Artists answer the unanswerable. Poetic ascent and philosophical belief require to be combined.

II

Religion is the direct apprehension of the Supreme. It is the attaining of a state of illumination. While the Reality is omnipresent, the human being is able to apprehend it directly in his own inmost being.[1] The principle is enunciated

[1] Samādhi is a state of consciousness, a frame of mind which consists in the highest concentration on the most concrete of all concrete things,

in the Upanisadic maxim, *tat tvam asi*, That art Thou. The fish in the water are thirsting and people in the world are roaming all over the world to seek the Divine, while they are all in the Divine, fragments of it. When we push our investigations in science, we are faced by a mystery. Beyond all that we can formulate about the self and its processes, there is the final mystery of the self that can never be known since it is always the knower, the centre of freedom and the bearer of responsibility.

When we reach the limits of scientific knowledge, we reach two mysteries—that which is within the self and that which is beyond the world. The Upaniṣad says that Atman is Brahman. The two are co-related. In and through one's freedom, we discover the real, we come most fully into possession of the self and feel that we are not our own, that we have been given the self as a sacred trust. This vision of reality is not an escape from reality but an encounter with reality in its depths.

Augustine establishes the possibility of certitude in general before establishing the certainty of God's existence. He does this by seizing upon the greatest of all certitudes, the certitude that even the sceptic's wildest doubts cannot shake, namely, his own existence. For even though a man does not yet know if God exists or not, he does know that he himself exists. Śaṁkara and

---

on the all-sustaining, immediate, concrete, unveiled reality. In this state, the individual human being participates in full measure in that illumination which far surpasses the thinking of a person who understands himself as the ego-consciousness. Ordinary language only hints at the direct truth of the reality which presents itself to one in this state.

Descartes adopt a similar view. The hidden treasure of the self is life in eternity which knows no bondage, decay or sorrow.

True Religion should be distinguished from mere knowledge of dogmas or ritualistic piety. Meditation is the way to self knowledge. Heaven is a state of one's spiritual being. It is up to each individual to attain harmony, awakening to spiritual truth. That state reflects truth and love, is one of compassion and forbearance.

All experiences which are called spiritual have certain characteristics in common. First, the experience is given. It cannot be induced by will or prolonged by effort. It does not answer the bidding of the will. It occurs when we least expect it for a fleeting moment no longer than the winking of an eye or the raising of the hand. The Indian scriptures compare the spiritual experience with a flash of lightning, which suddenly appears in the middle of a dark blue cloud.[1] The capacity of any individual to receive the experience may be affected by age, by psycho-physical make-up, and by cultural milieu. Though all men are capable of it, few put forth the effort needed for it. Secondly, whatever the contents of the experience the subject is absolutely convinced that it is a revelation of reality. It bears an authority within itself, an authority of unquestionable and immeasurable power. It is felt to be a revelation from the fountain of life itself. It is illumination, a state of being. There is a sense of release. Thirdly, since God is the 'wholly other', human language is not an adequate means for expressing it. The kind of knowledge we

[1] *nīlatoyada-madhyastha vidyul-lekheva bhāsvarā.*

have of objects existing independently of us is different from the kind of knowledge we have of other persons with whom we are involved, while there is extreme articulateness with regard to the objects, there is inarticulateness with regard to persons. The direct apprehension of Reality is incommunicable. 'Whether in the body, I cannot tell; or whether out of the body, I cannot tell: God knoweth.'[1] Jacques Maritain writes, 'The more he knows God, either by reason or by faith, the more he understands that our concepts attain (through analogy) but do not circumscribe Him, and that his thoughts are not like our thoughts: for who hath known the mind of the Lord or who hath become his counsellor?[2] The more strong and deep faith becomes, the more man kneels down, not before his own alleged ignorance of truth, but before the inscrutable mystery of divine truth and before the hidden ways in which God goes to meet those who search Him.'[3] The individual feels that reality was revealed to him, which in the normal state is hidden from him. Fourthly, with whatever the experience is concerned—things or human beings, or God—they are experienced as numinous, clothed in glory, charged with an intensity of being, an intense being-thereness. God is deep within us, around us, below us, above us, and beyond us. It is a being mighty and terrible and yet intimate and near. Lastly, the experience is so important that it completely absorbs the attention of the subject,

[1] II Corinthians, XII, 2.
[2] *Isaiah.* XL. 13.
[3] *The Graduate Journal,* Vol. III, No. 2. Fall 1960, p. 279.

so that his self, with his desires and needs, is of no importance whatever. While the vision lasts the self is completely forgotten.

IV

Encounter with Reality is possible only for those who have attained integration and harmony by overcoming the conflicts within themselves. Religion is the remaking of oneself. The human being requires to be renewed. He must be born again to enter the kingdom of heaven, of spirit. He must give up the material view of life. Jesus told Nicodemus, 'That which is born of the flesh is flesh and that which is born of the spirit is spirit. Marvel not that I said unto thee, ye must be born again.'[1] We must wake up to the reality of the kingdom of spirit. Religion helps to free the sleeping forces of the enslaved spirit. It awakens the real in man and recreates the Being itself.

Of this rebirth St Paul says: 'You must not fall in with the manners of this world; there must be an inward change, a remaking of your mind, so that you can satisfy yourselves what is God's will, the good thing, the desirable thing, the perfect thing.'[2]

Man realizes his finitude as he is overcome by anxiety between the *a priori* knowledge of his essential being and the awfulness of the possibility of his non-being. What gives hope is that in the awareness of his finitude is found the awareness of his potential infinity. This awareness of potential infinity leads to a knowledge

[1] *John* VII. 6–7.
[2] *Romans* XII. 2.

of eternality. Man, realizing his position of estrangement from the ground of Being (the Absolute), struggles for re-unification with it.

'Mind is said to be of two types: the pure and the impure. It is impure when it is subject to the pressures of lust, and pure when free from them.'[1] When we cleanse ourselves and attain a status of perfect integrity, we become divinized in our being. For St Paul, he who 'is the image of the Invisible God' created all 'things visible and things invisible'.[2] The phrase 'image of God' is used, in the Greek Old Testament, of the Divine wisdom.[3] St Paul applies to Christ a description of one of the intermediaries, which had been introduced in later Hebrew thought, to relate the transcendental Absolute, and the world of his making. In one passage St Paul says that Christ is the wisdom of God[4], and wisdom in the Old Testament is both the pre-existent principle[5] and the artificer of creation.[6] To be saved, to be liberated from the trammels of time, one has to realize this 'wisdom'. Each one has to realize for himself, unveil the God in him. 'Work out your own salvation with fear and trembling.'[7]

According to the Fourth Gospel the purpose of the Incarnation is the revelation, the giving of light, the revealing of God and man as they should be, according to the divine plan. It is the com-

[1] *mano hi dvividham proktam śuddhaṁ cāśuddham eva ca-aśuddhaṁ kāma-samparkāt śuddhaṁ kāma-vivarjitam.*

Pañcadaśī, XI. 116.

[2] *Colossians* I. 15–16.
[3] *Wisdom* VII. 26.
[4] *Corinthians* I. 24–30.
[5] *Proverbs* VIII. 23.
[6] *Proverbs* VIII. 30.
[7] *Philippians* II. 12

munication of life, the life of the age to come.[1]

Justin Martyr says that 'the power sent from the Father' is called 'the Word because he brings messages from the Father to men'.[2] There are those who regard the Word as the principle of rationality. He is the Word of whom every race of men were partakers, and those who lived with the Word are Christians, even though they have been thought atheists.[3]

V

We discriminate between authentic experiences and spurious ones by their conformity with knowledge attained by other means and ethical fruitfulness. 'Do not believe every spirit but test the spirits whether they are of God.'[4] The soul who has the experience is a changed one. He is said to be a reborn soul. He sees the divine underlying the whole universe. The emancipated soul, it is said, seeks solitude, is detached from the bonds binding one to the world, is raised above the three qualities of *sattva* (serenity) *rajas* (passion) and *tamas* (inertia), is devoted to the progress and prosperity of the world, gives up interest in the fruits of work, is detached from work, is lifted above the distinction of good and evil, renounces even the scriptures, is always lost in God.[5]

[1] *Wisdom* IX. 2.

[2] *Dialogue* I. 28.

[3] *Apology*, I, XLVI.

[4] *John* IV. 1.

[5] *yo viviktaṁ sthānaṁ sevate, yo loka-bandhanaṁ unmūlayati, nistraiguṇyo bhavati, yo yogakṣemam bhajati, yaḥ karma-phalam tyajati, karmāṇi saṁnyasyati, tato nirdvando bhavati, yo vedān api saṁnyasyati kevalam avicchinnānurāgam labhate.*

Gregory the Great says: 'Holy men discern between illusion and revelations, the very words and images of visions, by a certain inward sensibility, so that they know what they receive from the good spirit and what they endure from the deceiver. For, if a man's mind were not careful in this regard, it would plunge itself into many vanities through the deceiving spirit, who is sometimes wont to foretell many true things, in order that he may entirely prevail to ensnare the soul by some one single falsity.'[1] Meister Eckhart in his *Sermons* says, 'The reborn soul is as the eye, which, having gazed into the sun thenceforward sees the sun in everything'. It is humble, and does not think more than it is; it is loving, because it does not tend to love only itself; it is truthful, because it sets aside its own tastes and prejudices. When harmony is established, the self is said to be born; that is, the immortal spirit which had formerly been hidden manifests itself. It is the integration of personality. It is to realize the totality of the self without the loss of ego-consciousness. It is the revelation of timeless being in oneself, without losing the consciousness of time. It is a godlike condition.[2]

VI

Indian thought does not disregard individual human life or condemn individuals to utter insignificance. Maturity and strength do not mean hardening into an impervious, possessive,

[1] *See* C. G. Jung: *Collected Works,* Vol. II (1958), p. 20.

[2] Angelus Silesius spoke of the birth of the son of God in the soul of man.

self-assertive personality, but the inner purification and illumination of human existence, so that it can be in accord with ultimate truth and Reality. A truly religious man lives on the frontiers between the sacred and the secular, between religion and politics, between being and non-being. We are not called upon to get out of history and get into the desert and lead lives of renunciation and resignation. The saintly participate in the work of the world and push it forward. Their every word is a prayer; their every deed a sacrifice. Men of saintliness belong to one religion. Whatever line of activity we adopt, there is the road to fulfilment. The question of the attainment of the goal of life depends, in the last resort, on our spirit of earnestness. All life is great and leads to purity. Greatness lies in worthy living among the common things of life. Gāndhi writes, 'If I seem to take part in politics, it is only because politics today encircle us like the coils of a snake from which one cannot get out, no matter how one tries. I wish to wrestle with the snake . . . I am trying to introduce religion into politics.'[1]

Religions will lose their redemptive power, if saintly lives are not encouraged. No institutional patterns, no sophisticated theologies, can atone for inward spiritual poverty. The quality of our life is the evidence of our religion. The saints offer us encouragement and rebuke, not by their bearing blamelessness or effortless superiority but by the ease with which they face the risks and temptations of life. They make it easy for us to believe in goodness, though we do not take them seriously, for we

[1] *Young India,* May 2, 1920.

do not determine our conduct by their standards.

A holy man is said to be somewhat inhuman, remote and harsh to the sinners. Those who are most close to the Divine are most human and compassionate. They are full of joy and hope for the world and do not wither into sadness or cynicism.

It is not correct to regard saintly persons as unworldly beings with a certain gloom and grimness about their behaviour.[1] Sanctity does not mean aloofness or withdrawal from the world. It is purity of spirit, undefeated by all that threatens or opposes it. It is creative goodness in the midst of evil, bringing with it healing. Nor does sanctity mean a cloistered life.

Self-control is the quality which marks the great contemplatives. They give up things which are said to be precious according to worldly standards to gain something more precious. Freed from personal desires, ambitions, possessions, they bear witness to a world better than the one in which anger, jealousy, greed rage.

It is not possible to be completely cut off from the world. God is everywhere and there is no place where God is not. If there is opposition between God and the world, a complete withdrawal from the world is the only way of escape. 'If I ascend up into heaven, thou art there; if I make my bed in hell, behold, thou art there,' says the Psalmist. We should be detached from the evil of the world.[2]

[1] Dean Inge said that he would not mind if someone did not call him a saint but he would feel hurt if someone said that he was not a gentleman.

[2] *cf:* 'I am not asking that Thou shouldst take them out of the world, but that Thou shouldst keep them clear of what is evil. They do not belong to the world, as I, too, do not belong to the world.'

John XVII. 15–16.

We must work in the world with meekness and humility of heart. We must live fully in the world and love it deeply, when we can point beyond it to the depths of its reality and the richness of the eternal.

Saintliness is not a prerogative of any one religion. Trappist monasteries are found in the United States. Cistercian monks practise rigorous discipline. They rise at a very early hour in the morning, spend eight hours a day in prayer, do not eat meat, fish or eggs, do not speak except to their superiors, do not leave the monastery and rarely see visitors. There are twenty such Trappist monasteries in the United States, most of them founded since the last war, an astonishing challenge to all the material values that some of us too easily identify with the United States. They are contemplatives cut off from the world but yet affect the world. Their prayer, silence, devotion and work are offered in some measure to counteract the cruelty, pain and senselessness outside their walls.

In early Christianity, social service was not encouraged as a result of eschatological expectations. So those who believed that the existent order would shortly give way to a final judgment, family life, property and even self-preservation seemed unimportant. The Christian alienation from the world survived the non-fulfilment of its eschatological hopes. The other-worldliness was independent of the belief in the perishability of the world.

In all religions there are a few who show their superiority to nature by leading ascetic lives.

VII

In Indian thought, though saints are exalted, the

normal code is fulness of life. *Dharma*, *artha*, *kāma* and *mokṣa* form the supreme ends of life. All human relationships are to be fitted into a spiritual pattern. *Kāma* includes harmony and happiness in sex life. Freedom is essential in it. By force of will, we cannot express effectively and co-operate, when one feels cross and resentful. We take vows of celibacy but we are far from being celibate.

Sex is a social phenomenon. Even primitive tribes subject sex to social regulations. We require some moral habits, if we are to fulfil the demands of our average existence. The regulations are necessary for our normal life. If they are regarded as absolute, they will become destructive. Adam was asked not to eat of the tree of knowledge. If Adam had been one with his true being, the negative command would not have been necessary. As a human being, he had the freedom to contradict his true being. In the condition of temptation, he had already violated his true being.

In the absence of law there is no sin. With the rise of law, the possibility of sin appears. With full self scrutiny, we may violate the law and be prepared for the consequences. For human beings, sex life is to be blended with intelligence and imagination. Love is not a mere impulse of curiosity or a leap of lust. It is spiritual in character.

For the Greeks, romantic passion is a temporary derangement of the senses. By the time of Propertius, this passion was an established phenomenon. In Augustan Rome there was no sense of guilt about sex.

The Christian teaching about sex is that it is usually wrong but can, in view of the fragility of human nature, be 'excused' in marriage, to use the words of Pope Gregory.[1]

Under the influence of Pauline theology, Christianity developed into an anti-erotic religion. St Paul believes that human love detracts from the love of God, even if it does not stand in active rivalry to it. The destruction of Pompeii came to be regarded by some Christians as God's vengeance on an evil and lascivious people.

Moral habits die hard. It is not right to say that we are all wanting to be freed from the chains of prejudice. We prefer captivity to freedom. Even when the prison doors fly open, we choose to remain in our cells and do not wish to escape. For the hold of tradition is strong. Our contempt for the flesh becomes a type of militant chastity.

Sex is something sacred and not dirty. If religion is real, it must hallow one's whole life. To rejoice in love, to love children, to love where love is, are real and good. 'With my body I thee worship.' When we say that love is blind and it sees no fault in the beloved, that blindness is the deepest sight.

Kant asks us to subordinate the senses, the natural impulses and passions to reason and law. It is not subordinating impulses to reason but a harmony of reason and impulse. Our generation is out of joint where relations of men and women are concerned.

Mr Young in his *Eros Denied* says: 'Among the great religions of the world Christianity must be squarely qualified as anti-life. Its repressive attitude in regard to sex causes more suffering to believers and alienates potential converts than all other attitudes put together.'

[1] *cf:* St Paul: 'It is better to marry than to burn.'

In many countries, especially in the East, attempts are being made to bring down population by artificial means. The religious object to these plans. St Augustine reasoned persuasively: 'intercourse even with one's legitimate wife is unlawful and wicked, where the conception of offspring is prevented. Onan, the son of Juda, did this and the Lord killed him for it.'[1] Production of offspring is not the only aim of marriage. The growth of mutual love in the partners is also the aim of marriage, perhaps the main aim.

At Vatican Council II, sexual life was recognized as a natural phenomenon which contributes to human happiness. Cardinals Suenens and Leger and many others held that 'though the institution of matrimony itself and conjugal love are ordained for the procreation and education for children, and find in them their ultimate crown,' still conjugal love 'is uniquely expressed and perfected through the marital act. The actions within marriage by which the couple are united intimately and chastely are noble and worthy ones'. Apart from procreation, conjugal love has an independent value.

Our women's world is less heterogeneous and more natural than the man's world. Women have a beneficent influence on man's work and leisure. Kant held that woman should hold herself aloof from politics. This does not mean that there should be any diminution of the principle of social equality. The masculinizing of women will deprive them of their essentially feminine nature. Even in politics, they should not overlook their specific graces and gifts.

[1] *De aduterinis coningiia,* II. 12.

One of the main tests of the degree of civilization attained by a society is the way it treats its women. She is said to be *abalā*, the weaker, physically perhaps, though not in other ways.

CHAPTER VI

THE FELLOWSHIP OF RELIGIONS

I

At no other time in history has mankind been more alive to the need for human co-operation. Religions, hitherto, have been building walls between one another instead of breaking down barriers. The ecumenical movement is growing and the United Nations Declaration of Human Rights adopted in 1948 contains a provision to foster religious freedom.[1] Freedom of religion is enjoyed by the citizens of many countries and protected by their constitutions and laws. The Roman Catholic Church now admits that every person has the right to worship God, according to his conscience, subject only to the moral law and the maintenance of public order. It allows the right to hold differing views.

No one is so vain of his religion as he who knows no other. If we know the classics of other religions, we will admire them and share their joys and sorrows. Advocates of religion sometimes become missionaries of hatred towards other religions. This

[1] Articles 18 and 19 of the Declaration read thus:

Article 18: Everyone has the right to freedom of thought, conscience and religion; this right includes freedom to change his religion or belief, and freedom, either alone or in community with others and in public or private, to manifest his religion or belief in teaching, practice, worship and observance.

Article 19: Everyone has the right to freedom of opinion and expression; this right includes to hold opinions without interference and to seek, receive and impart information and ideas through any media and regardless of frontiers.

is something inconsistent with the spirit of true religion. In an age of acute religious conflict, Hugo Grotius asserted that 'there was no sense at all in Catholics and Protestants seeking to impose their special dogmas upon each other; and that, if only they would *think* quietly, instead of *feeling* wildly, humanity would be relieved of much meaningless wastage and much atrocious suffering'. The fanaticism of the religious as well as that of the anti-religious may not breed wars but they still use the weapons of hate, misrepresentation, distortion and suppression.

The Upaniṣads frequently refer to the Real as the Supreme Self, *param-ātman*. Two birds, companions (who are) always united, cling to the self-same tree. Of these two, the one eats the sweet fruit and the other looks on without eating.[1] The Divine companion is always with us and in us. All religions bear witness to the penetration of the finite by the infinite. We see the universal through the concrete. 'The One Luminous, the maker of all, the great self always dwelling in the hearts of people, revealed through love, intuition, intelligence. Whoever knows him becomes immortal.'[2] Reality is immutable but human apprehension of it is mutable, changing.

Every religion is based on a personal encounter, a human apprehension and all theologies are stam-

[1] *dvā suparṇā sayujā sakhāyā samānaṁ*
vṛkṣam pariṣasvajāte
tayor anyaḥ pippalaṁ svādv atty anaśnann
anyo 'bhicākaśīti.

Muṇḍaka Upaniṣad III. I. 1.

See also *Kaṭha Upaniṣad* I. 3, 1. *Śvetāśvatara Upaniṣad* IV. 6.

[2] *esa devo viśvakarmā mahātmā sadā janānām hṛdaye sannivistaḥ*
hṛdā manīśā manasābhiklpto ya evam viduḥ amṛtas ta bhavanti.

mering attempts to translate the experience into words and draw out its implications. The majesty of God, the mysery of reality is so great that human language is inadequate to describe it. It is unutterable and incommunicable. Plato expresses doubt about the validity of any description of the Ultimate Reality. 'There does not exist, there never shall, any treatise by myself on these matters. The subject does not admit, as the sciences in general do, of exposition. It is only after long association in the great business itself and a shared life, that a light breaks out in the soul, kindled, so to say, by a leaping flame, and thereafter feeds itself.'[1] The prayer of Nicholas of Cusa testifies to this truth. 'O, Lord My God, the helper of them that seek Thee, I behold Thee in the entrance of Paradise and I know not what I see, for I see naught visible. This alone I know, that I know not what I see, and never can know. And I know not how to name Thee, because I know not what Thou art and did anyone say unto me that Thou wert called by this name or that, by the very fact that he named it, I should know that it was not Thy name. For the wall beyond which I see Thee, is the end of all manner of signification in names. Nothing is quite true; perhaps even this is not quite true.' Hafiz says that nobody has ever solved and nobody will ever solve the eternal riddle.

II

The Absolute is Being. *Exodus* records that God replied to Moses, 'I AM that I AM.' 'Before Abraham was, I AM.' The world exists. It need

[1] *Epistle* VII.

not have existed. Existence is the expression of Being over non-being. The existential being takes us to the essential being. The world takes us to Being, which has its mark on everything, and we have but to observe things to be led from them to Being. Being and creative power, stillness and motion spring from the same source Being, Self. Heaven is not up above but is in us. 'The kingdom of God cometh not with observation. Neither shall they say, 'lo here or lo there' for behold, the kingdom of God is within you.'[1] Zen Buddhism rejects God as he is manifest in phenomena. It detaches itself from the manifestations in order to find the Real in his non-manifestation.

The non-dogmatic character of the Hindu religion comes out in the famous vedic hymn:

'Non-existent there was not, existent there was not then. There was not space, nor the vault beyond. What stirred, where, and in whose control? Was there water, a deep abyss?

'Nor death nor immortality was there then; there was no distinction of night or day. That One breathed without breath by inner power; than it, verily, there was nothing else further.

'Darkness there was, hidden by darkness, in the beginning; an undistinguished ocean was this All. What generative principle was enveloped by emptiness—by the might of (its own) fervour That One was born.

'Desire arose then in the beginning, which was the first seed of thought. The connection of the existent the sages found in the non-existent, searching with devotion in their hearts.'

Again, 'Who truly knows? Who shall here pro-

[1] *Luke* X, VII. 20.

claim it—whence they were produced, whence this creation? The gods arose on this side (later), by the creation of this (empiric world, to which the gods belong); then who knows whence it came into being? whether it was established, or whether not —he who is its overseer in the highest heaven, he verily knows, perchance he knows not.' *Tao Teh-Ching* says: 'Looked at, it cannot be seen; listened to, it cannot be heard.' Concepts are used as symbols the value of which lies not in their literal meaning but in their suggestiveness. They should be treated in the spirit not of logic but of poetry. When we emphasize the ineffable character of the Reality, its transcendence of subject-object relation, we call it the Absolute. When we look at it, as the creative principle of all existence, we conceive it as God. The Absolute and God are two statuses of the same Reality. Both these aspects are found in Buddhism. There is the Absolute, the supra-existential state described as voidness, *śūnyatā*. It is nothing compared to the plenitude of existence, *saṁsāra*. It is also the Divine with reference to its cosmic manifestations. Blissful voidness which is the ontological reality is also personified as the boundless compassion of the Buddha. The voidness has taken a doctrinal form in Mahāyāna and an expressionist aspect in Zen Buddhism of which Bodhi-dharma is the inaugurator. Vimalakīrti, in the sūtra which bears his name, answers Bodhisattva Manjuśrī's question about the nature of reality with a thunderlike silence.

St Gregory Palamas teaches that God contains Being without being reducible to it. For Eckhart God is 'Being above Being and super-essential negation'. For Boehme, the Supreme is the ground and abyss of being.

Every belief in Ultimate Reality as God is restrictive in character. It fixes limits, boundaries. The assumption of a personal God as the ground of being and creator of the universe is the first stage of the obscuring and restriction of the vision which immediately perceives the great illumination of Reality. It permits the knowledge of the truth that ever transcends God, does not annihilate God but comprises it.

When we say God is truth we mean that he is the primordial fact or reality and we should worship him in spirit and in truth. Truth is never preached for one has to realize it within oneself. One cannot know the Supreme except in part only for the Supreme comprises all things, the seen and the unseen, the manifest and the unmanifest.

Masnavi says: 'The moon is not in the stream but in the sky.' It means that the Reality is outside and beyond the phenomenal world. It is not the transient reflection. The mirror depends on the original and owes all to it. The original stands in no need of the mirror. A Sūfi saint said: 'There are as many ways to God as there are human hearts.' All honest striving is sacred.

III

There are many descriptions of God. They are points of view and not objects of knowledge. For the Greeks, God is absolute reality, spirit. The Latin theologians regard God with the mind of the Roman warrior, as a governor, law giver. Not content with his eternity, God intervenes in the affairs of earth. He is sometimes represented as subject to human passions. He disconcerts, irritates, seduces. He shrieks, storms and castigates. He dispenses justice according to his whims. There is no code to control his impulses. God in many religions is an aggressive despot, full of phobias and complexes. Paul Tillich rejects the God of traditional theism in favour of a 'God above God' who is the 'ground of all being' and the source of man's 'ultimate concern'. Bishop Robinson likewise rejects the traditional notion of a God 'out there' who exists 'above and beyond the world he made'. They repudiate anthropomorphism.

When we hold to the imaginative pictures of the Divine with fervour, we tend to become intolerant. Hatred is the product of intolerance, and persecutions are born of hatred. Antisemitism arose out of the story of the crucifixion of Jesus by a Jew, a misunderstanding two thousand years old. From Nebuchadnezzar to Hitler, the Jews were condemned and the same terms were used as by Tacitus who says: 'Moses, the better to bind the nation to himself instituted new rites, contrary to those of all other mortals. Here all that we worship is flouted: in return all that is impure in our eyes is allowed.' On the other hand, the Jews affirm that they had a special role in God's dealings with the world. God chose the Jews to be the special people and revealed to them through prophets and law givers the truth about himself. Jesus was born among the Jews.

The world of Heraclitus is in the Logos of Christianity. The word made flesh is wisdom given human expression. Irenaeus holds that Jesus came and lived the life of man in order that man might live a life comparable to that of Jesus. Man is redeemed from corruption or guilt as the later theologians put it.

Many different ways were devised to relate Jesus and the Godhead. Origen stressed the eternal generation of the Son. This means that since the Son was begotten in eternity, which by definition is outside time, there can be no beginning or ending to the process. Arius, about 319 AD, argues that the Son is creature, the first and most perfect of God's creatures but nevertheless he is made by God. As the human son is subsequent to the father in time so is the divine son of later existence than the divine Father. Here Arius carries Origen's subordinationism to its logical extreme. The Council of Nicea (325) condemned Arius and affirmed that the Son was 'begotten, not made and that he was of one substance with the Father'. The Cappadocian trio, St Basil of Caesarea, his brother St Gregory of Nyasa and their friend, St Gregory of Nazianus, explain how one God can nevertheless be at the same time three. They taught that Godhead is one being but of this one Being there are three objective presentations: Father, Son and Holy Spirit: These three are distinguished from one another by their individual characteristics which are in fact modes of existence. The Father as the fount and source of deity is un-begotten; the son is begotten and the Spirit is proceeding.[1] These three processes take place in eternity. It is difficult, says St Gregory of Nazianus 'to conceive God but to define him in words is an impossibility.'[2] St Augustine said, 'for the sake of

[1] *cf: John* I. 14; XV. 26.
[2] *Orations* XXVIII. 4.

speaking of things ineffable, that in some way we may be able to express what we are in no way able to express fully, our Greek friends have spoken of one essence and three substances but the Latins of one essence or substance and three persons.' He thinks that either position is legitimate for 'the transcendence of the Godhead surpasses the power of ordinary speech'.[1] The doctrine of the Trinity is an attempt to correlate the truths of these Christian experiences of God, but it does not explain everything.

These are all attempts to express the economy in the internal organization of the Godhead. We have the Reality which transcends all empirical characterization, the personal God who is the creator, saviour of the universe. We have the testimony of the saints to these two forms of Godhead. When it is said that 'I am the way and the truth and the life,' 'No one comes to the father but through me,'[2] it means that normally we reach the super-personal through the personal.

The living faiths themselves are in disorder. If we wish to restore order, we should wake up to a full consciousness of our conditions and see where we are.

In the varied imaginative representations of God, we have to glimpse a substantial being superior to the world. To speak of God as a person is merely conceptional, symbolic speaking. We overlook the fundamental fact that religion is the will of the creature to raise himself above himself through toil and effort. All people, religious or non-religious, have this urge. Every generation tries to rediscover authentic human values and oppose

[1] *cf: The Trinity* VII. 7.
[2] *John* XIV. 6.

the forms of stagnation, which, in each generation man invents to increase his own misery. We must get to terms with death and be liberated into true living that comes from the acceptance of death.

God is not a being who interferes with the universe to set aside natural laws. He allows them to function in a normal way. We cannot accept the view that God sends to us sickness and disaster. God is the deepest in us which we have to get at through prayer and meditation. The '*Acts of Peter*' say of Christ: 'Thou art unto me father, thou my mother, thou my brother, thou my friend, thou my bondsman, thou my steward. Thou art All and All is in thee; thou Art, and there is naught else that is save thee only.

'Unto him therefore do ye also, brethren, flee, and if ye learn that in him alone ye exist, ye shall obtain those things whereof he saith unto you: Which neither eye hath seen nor ear heard, neither have they entered into the heart of man.'[1] These are echoes of familiar hymns to God in the Śaiva, Śākta and Vaiṣṇava systems.

Faith, adoration, prayer, love quicken man's consciousness, so that it knows the Supreme more than it does before. Man looks towards him, aspires to him, prays to him and loves him. Jesus was so humble that he said, 'The words that I speak unto you I speak not myself; but the Father that dwelleth in me, he doeth the works.'[2]

Śraddhāvān labhate jnānam. Śraddhā is humility, reverence, devotion. It is neither self-abasement nor self-exaltation. It is self-effacement and dedication to a purpose. It is simplicity, it is self-

[1] E.T. James, p. 335.
[2] *John* XIV. 10.

reliance, it is absence of conceit and arrogance. The path is through sacrifice and renunciation. 'Not mine but thy will be done.' We wish to establish the kingdom of God on earth. St Paul asks us to pray without ceasing. The whole life of saints is, according to Origen, 'one single great continuing prayer'. Its reward is not only the ascent of man to God but the revelation of God in the heart of man.

Zarathustra's chief teaching is that we fill our mind with good thoughts, good words and good deeds. Rituals and ceremonies are an escape from these. Spiritual experience is related in religious books by writers who explored the frontiers of spirit in different conditions at remote times and in many languages. One shock of recognition unites the whole world. We must recover the lost sense of community, get rid of hatred, rancour and intolerance, recognize the super-natural reality in which we are all one.

The saint's life is not complete in the contemplative life. Service to brethren, the active life is also there. The Buddha, after enlightenment, out of compassion for all suffering beings, preached the sacred truth to all men. Meister Eckhart declared that if some one in the highest rapture noticed a poor man in need of soup, it is better for him to forego his rapture and serve the man in need. All religions ask us to practise brotherly love. Love is inseparable from knowledge. Goodness and all encompassing care are the characteristics of Tao. The inmost essence of Divine Reality is *mahā-karuṇā-cittaṁ* according to Mahāyāna Buddhism, this heart is open to all men. Even as the light of the moon is reflected in every kind of water, muddy or clear, river, lake or ocean, so is the divine heart of love revealed to all mankind, high or low, saint or sinner. *Hadith* of the prophet says: 'When the servant takes one step towards his Lord, the Lord gets up from his throne and takes one hundred steps to meet his servant.'

Samarpaṇa, ātma-nivedana, the spirit of dedication, marks the religious life. We must have a purpose, a cause to live for and die for. It is this lack of purpose that is making our lives fitful, casual, meaningless. The self-assertive conceit and meaningless arrogance of many self-satisfied people are traceable to the lack of wisdom, holiness and sanity. Dedication should not lapse into decay, enthusiasm should not end in frustration.

'He that is slow to anger is better than the mighty; and he that ruleth his spirit than he that taketh a city.'[1] Self-control helps us to harmonize our life.

We have today not a confrontation of religions but a meeting of them. Fifty years ago, it would have been a betrayal of one's faith to seek to find what is valuable in other religions. There are representative leaders of different living faiths pledged to mutual understanding. They stress the common aim of religions and not the things which separate them. No religion today cares to live on mere revival or repetition of the past. All religions stress the common inheritance and plead for progress along a path of mutual respect and understanding. We feel that we are all partners in the same quest.

The meeting together of the religions has contributed to the vitality of these religions. Religious

[1] *Proverbs* XVI. 23.

isolationism is no longer possible. It is today one of the responsibilities of a student of religion to understand the existence of other religions, each with its own specific structure and background, with its own claims. The different religious traditions are governed by the same spirit, and work for the redemption of both man and the universe. Cosmic salvation is the aim of all religions.

The different names we give to the Supreme apply to the one Supreme.

'You, O Agni, are Varuṇa when you are born. You become Mitra when you are kindled. In you, O son of strength, are all gods. You are Indra for the pious mortal.' Again, the different names Brahma, Viṣṇu, Śiva, are given to the One with reference to the three functions of creation, maintenance and dissolution.[1] All the religions of the world, at their best, require us to understand one another in a spirit of humility and friendliness. Whatever helps us to get a living sensation of the Supreme is permitted.

The Vedas ask the peoples of the earth to walk together, to talk together and think together to secure peace on earth. Gāndhi tells us: 'I do not believe in the exclusive divinity of the Vedas. I believe the Bible, the Koran and the Zend-Avesta to be as divinely inspired as the Vedas . . . Hinduism is not a missionary religion. In it there is room for the worship of all the prophets in the world . . . Hinduism tells every one to worship God according to his own faith or dharma, and so it lives in peace

[1] *ekasya kasyacid aśeṣa-jagat-prasūti-hetor anādi-puruṣasya mahā-vibhuteḥ*
ṣṛṣti-sthiti-pralaya-kārya-vibhāga-yogād brahmeti viṣṇur iti rudra iti pratītiḥ.

Nyayamañjari, I. 242 (Jayantabhatta).

with all religions.'[1] Buddha declares: 'Never think or say that your own religion is the best. Never denounce the religion of others . . . rather honour whatever in them is worthy of honour.' The *Talmud* says: 'The pious of all nations shall have a share in the life to come.' The *New Testament* says: God hath made of one blood all nations of men.'[2] 'Verily, whether it be of those who believe or those who are Jews or Christians or Sabaeans, whosoever believe in God and the last day and act aright, they have their reward at their Lord's hand, and there is no fear for them, nor shall they grieve.'[3] All these call upon us to build a world unity without strife and hatred. Let us transform this common interest into a unity of purpose.

Hindu thought believes in the reality of One which is described in different ways. The duality assumed for the sake of devotion is more beautiful than even non-duality.'[4] Starting from crude modes of worship the devotee should progress to nobler modes. The first stage is image worship; the next consists in meditation and prayer; still higher is mental worship; the meditation which is of the form 'I am he' is the highest.[5] The different traditions found in India were all respectfully

[1] *cf:* 'All religions are like different roads leading to the same goal.' (*Hind Swaraj.*)

'All religions are founded on the same moral laws. My ethical religion s made up of laws which bind men all over the world.' (*Ethical Religion.*)

[2] *Acts* XVII. 26.

[3] *Qurán Sura* II. 59.

[4] *bhaktyartham kalpitaṁ dvaitam*
advaitād api sundaram.

[5] *prathamā pratimā pūjā*
japa-stotrāṇi madhyamā
uttamā mānasi pūjā
só ham pūjottamottamā.

accepted and justified.[1] Vedic and Tantrik are the two schools prevalent in India. Tantra is what saves and amplifies.[2] 'Looking from the body-level, I am God's servant; from the level of the individual soul functioning through the mind, I am a part or aspect of God; but from the aspect of my *ātmā* (or pure self) I am one with God. That is my definite conviction.'[3] The same idea is found also in Vidyāranya's *Saṁkara Vijaya.*[4] A Hindu writer says, At heart I am a Śākta, outwardly a Śaiva and in gatherings a Vaiṣṇava.[5] Brahmā, Viṣṇu and Śiva are one. The *Amṛitabindu upaniṣad* says that we should ascend the aumkāra chariot with Viṣṇu as the charioteer, worship Rudra and get to Brahma-loka.[6]

In the world where Hinduism and Buddhism

[1] *cf:* Kullūka Bhaṭṭa:

'Vaidikī tāntrikī caiva
dvividhā śrutir īritā.'

[2] *tanyate vistāryate.*

[3] *deha buddhyā tu dāsohaṁ*
jiva buddhyā tvadaṁśakaṁ
ātma buddhyā tvam evāhaṁ
iti me niścitā matiḥ.

[4] *dāsaste'haṁ deha-buddhyā 'smi śaṁbho*
jātastvaṁso jīva buddhyā tridṛṣṭe
sarvasyātmann-ātmadṛṣṭyā tvameve' ty evaṁ
me dhī niścitā sarvaśāstraiḥ.

Ch. VI, Verse 41.

cf: Appaya Diksita who holds that there is no metaphysical distinction between Maheśvara and Janārdana.

'Maheśvare vā jagatām adhiśvare
janārdane vā jagad antarātmani
na vastu-bheda-pratipattir asti me
tathāpi bhaktir tarunenduśekhare.'

[5] *antaḥ śākto bahiḥ śaivo sabhāmadhye ca.*
vaiṣṇavaḥ.

[6] *aumkāra ratham āruhya*
viṣṇum kṛtva'tha sārathim
brahma-lokam avāpnoti
rudrārādhana tatparaḥ.

dominate, friendly co-operation and co-existence seem to be natural. With the rise of nuclear weapons the need for co-operation has become urgent. It is essential to understand other religions, appreciate their values and co-operate with them for the sake of self-preservation, if not out of higher considerations. Judaism, Christianity and Islam are less intransigent than ever before towards other religions. We now adopt a tentative attitude towards our own faith. We admit the limitations of the human mind and its inadequacy at least to know the inner truth. Even though one is tempted to exaggerate the exclusive adequacy to truth of one's own religion, we know now that others have the same feelings towards their own religions and put forth similar claims. We are all aware of the fallibility of the human mind. Besides, it is not easy to admit that God has been partial to a fraction of humanity. He cannot be conceived to have favourites. If God is love, he is the creator of all his creatures and must have revealed himself to all. So all revelations are to be admitted as having validity.

There is a growing sense of unity in Christendom today. Followers of the Church of England, Presbyterian, Methodist, Baptist and Free churches are able to get together and discuss vital problems among themselves. A Secretariat established in the Vatican under the chairmanship of Cardinal Bea is seeking a sense of unity among all Christians, whatever their persuasions may be. The encounter between the Archbishop of Canterbury, Dr Ramsey, and the present Pope marks a new stage in the development of fraternal relations based upon Christian charity, and of sincere efforts to remove the causes of conflict and to re-establish unity 'forgetting those things that are behind and reaching forth into those things which are before'.[1] We should press towards the goal of unity in truth. Karl Barth, the Protestant theologian, has become unsure of his original belief. He says, 'Nowadays both sides are getting to know each other and look upon each other as being on the same level, whereas in the old days they hardly knew each other at all'. The iron curtain has broken down. This coming together is not due to religious indifferentism or the flowing tide of secularism. It is a sign of growing up, of greater maturity. Two thousand years in the time scale of history are not very long. This same spirit has to be extended to all those who have love of God in heart and regard the service of man as their primary obligation. It is very much to be hoped that in the age opening out before us, intolerance and bigotry will diminish and fellowship and harmony will grow.

The time has come for us to join in unity of spirit, a unity which embraces the richness in which religious realities which have found expression in other faiths are not destroyed but cherished as valued expression of the One truth. We understand the real and spontaneous impulses which led to the formulation of the different faiths. We stress the touch of human warmth, compassion and sympathy that pervade the works of the finer minds of the faiths. There is no future for man apart from the religious dimension. No one with a knowledge of the comparative history of religion can retain an exclusive belief in the tenets of his own sect. We must enter into a dialogue with the

[1] *Philippians* III. 13.

world in which we labour. This does not mean that we work for a featureless unity of religions. We do not wish to lose the diversity which enshrines precious spiritual insight. Whether in family life, or lives of nations or religious life, it is a joining together of differences so that the integrity of each is preserved. Unity should be an intense reality and not a mere phrase. Man exposes himself to all the experiences of the future. Experiential religion is the religion of the future. It is that to which the fervent in the religious world is leading.

A study of other religions is essential for the understanding of one's own and is a valuable constituent of one's general culture. It is true that no one can master all the scriptures of the world. We must work for a new spiritual reconciliation and outlook in the light of recent developments with the aim of living together in harmony. The great prophets reveal to us the new being.[1]

[1] *cf:* Professor W. E. Hocking, who bases his hope for the coming world civilization on a partnership of the great religions, on 'the growing unity of their unlosable essences, the understanding acceptance of variety, and the quiet convergence of purpose in the identity of a historic task'.

The Coming World Civilisation.

CHAPTER VII

THE MEANING OF HISTORY

I

The ancient historians of the Graeco-Roman world, Thucydides, Herodotus, Tacitus, Livy, Plutarch, in spite of their aspiration to a scientific treatment of history admit that men determine history and so the study of human nature is of great importance to the historian.

Herodotus tells us that he wrote 'so that time may not blot out the memory of human achievement, and so that the great and remarkable deeds of the Greeks and the barbarians may not lack their meed of honour'. Tacitus seems to be interested more in the condemnation of evil than in the appreciation of virtue. He says, 'Never was it made more manifest that, while the gods care little for our well-being, they care greatly for our punishment'. Moral judgment assumes the freedom of the human individual, the power of the self, to choose one or the other of the alternatives. Nothing human can be calculated.

Man is the *kṣetra*, the field, where the strain between the actual and the ideal is to be endured. Hegel says, 'I am the struggle.' The human individual is the bearer of the spirit through which the higher world manifests itself. The king is the maker of history.[1] It is the duty of the king to provide the citizens with opportunities for spiritual growth. He should make them act with love whatever be the action.

[1] *rājā kālasya kāraṇam.*

The conflict between good and evil never ceases. It is never decided conclusively. If we do not obey the call of friendship, we are false to our nature. Love will prevail for man's fulfilment consists in following the lead of love. Human survival depends on the victory of wisdom and knowledge over stupidity and prejudice.

Human history is an indivisible whole. It is not a patchwork of unrelated episodes. Any fragment of history may not disclose meaning or purpose, but seen as a whole we find sense, meaning.

Those who have seen many catastrophes, so much of the world dissolve in ruin, are willing to agree with Goethe: 'World history: the most absurd thing there is!'

Human society consists of a network of human relations. It is not to be viewed as a mechanism. A human being is in certain aspects a mechanism, in others a biological organism, but in addition he has consciousness, the capacity for making choices. As an organism man is mortal, has a definite life span, but if a group comes to grief, it is man, the member of the group, that is held responsible. Those who insist on the primacy of the human spirit are convinced that mankind is steadily marching towards the realization of its highest aspirations, freedom of spirit and the rule of law.

We cannot say that the historical process is a movement towards any spiritual purpose. Ranke, the historian, felt, 'mankind bears within itself the seeds of many developments; they germinate one after another, and the great and mysterious laws which govern this process are hidden from our sight'. On this view, no historical epoch is a station on the road to the ultimate goal of history. In other words each epoch has its own purpose.

Belief in the progress of humanity towards a final goal is supported by man's mastery of science and technology. This concerns the external structure of our lives. The technological progress has no doubt enriched our lives, but it has also endangered them. But can we say that we have progress in philosophical pursuits? In wrestling with the great riddles posed by human existence, we do not discern much progress. The greatest attempts of philosophers do not go much beyond the thinking of previous centuries.

Has the role of morality in human affairs been effective? From the way nations are behaving, we do not discern any increase in commonsense. Lust for power and political, religious and economic domination seem to be the governing consideration. We cannot minimize the force of evil and believe in automatic progress. Progress is not a basic law of life. The contingency of history is due to the free choice of men. Every challenge we face, we do in the interests of harmony and freedom. The travail of history is the conflict between good and evil. We must fight the contradictions within and without us and fight the battle for truth and justice. There is no predetermined pattern. There is the play of the contingent, the unforeseen; the human will is unpredictable.

A human being is a social creature. To live he has to come to terms with the non-human environment and his fellow human beings. By mutual co-operation we have progressively mastered our non-human environment. We have not been equally successful in mastering the human environment. Here lies the tragedy. The advance of science and technology has widened the gulf between our intellectual progress and moral stagnation. If the human race is threatened with the doom of self-destruction, it is because of himself. Tools which can help to build an earthly paradise, if we are in harmony with each other, threaten annihilation, since we are fighting one another.

There is a feeling of disquiet in the world, because the world is in transition between an old order that is dying and a new that is struggling to be born. It is possible that there may be the death of the old order. We cannot be certain that there will be the birth of the new. History, so far as we know, is full of ups and downs. It is varied, wayward and uncertain. The freedom of the finite being is within limits. He is not free from conditions, biological, psychological and sociological. He is, however, free to resist these conditions and choose his attitude towards them. The future is open and the shape of things to come will depend on the choice which we will make. Those who have the mind to conceive and the sensibility to feel the disorder, the futility, the meaninglessness, the mystery of life and suffering can only find peace through a satisfaction of their whole being and the betterment of the world. Sensitive human beings will have to live through these experiments.

II

Time and timelessness, nature and supernature are twin aspects of man. He is both other-worldly and this-worldly, sacred and secular. Religion itself has a double direction, towards the timeless in adoration, towards the temporal in service. The

Bhagavadgītā asks us to meditate and act. We have to combine the *yoga* of *Kṛṣṇa,* contemplative insight, and the *dhanuṣ* of Arjuna, practical efficiency.

Religion is not a refuge from the world but an inspiration to act in the world. Man belongs to the world and the world beyond it. Spiritual life combines the active and the contemplative sides and transcends them. The way of the Cross is through the world of action. We grow from anguish to serenity, from doubt to faith in and through the world.

The Christian doctrine of Incarnation according to the Christians does not destroy time but raises it to an altogether new dimension. The Incarnation is the supreme act by which God intervened in human history to restore man's nature to its original integrity. The essential worth of man, however humble he may be, is the timeless element, the spirit in him which is the soul.

Freedom is the state of the unconditioned and the conditioned. The two are not distinct entities. *Nirvāṇa* and *Saṁsāra* are one. The descent which constitutes the great compassion, *mahā-karuṇa,* of the Buddhists, is, in reality, the realization of the non-duality of the conditioned and the unconditioned. The state of enlightenment is one of illumination and freedom as also of inexhaustible love which has for its object all sentient beings. It is manifested as uninterrupted activity in pursuit of the temporal and spiritual welfare of all beings.

In the twelfth century, an Italian abbot Joachim De Fiore expressed the view that there were three stages in history, of the Father in the Old Testament, of the Son in the thousand years of the

Christian era and the third stage of the Divine Spirit in which every one will be taught directly by the spirit, without the mediation of any organization. When social equality is established history may come to an end. In this age the spiritual man is the agent of history.

Man is not merely a casual product of mechanical processes, of nerves and complexes without any transcendental principle or self behind. The world cannot be regarded as a senseless play of blind forces. The universe has a meaning and man has a higher idea, which provides him with essential values which will save him from his present predicament. Man is not merely the apex of a process of natural evolution.

Metaphysical thinking, which bases itself on experience, holds that nature is grasped with the concept of necessity and the nature of the self by that of freedom. Without this concept, our understanding of man's nature will be deficient and distorted. While both man and nature are the creation of God, the being of man is made in the image of God,[1] and is therefore quite distinct from the being of nature. Man is not a *res cogitans* which, though distinct from *res extensa* is still a *res*, an objective concept and not the personal 'I'. We cannot understand man scientifically, as if he were only an unusually complicated object of nature. An objective account de-personalizes man and reduces him to a heterogeneous mass of fragments, which are studied by the different sciences. There is the biological man, the social man, the political man and also the individual man who feels pain and joy, bears responsibility, does good

[1] *Genesis.*

or evil, and is conscious of his alienation from himself, when he ceases to be subject and becomes an object.[1] 'I suffer, therefore, I am' is more correct than the Cartesion *'Cogito ergo sum'*, I think, therefore I am. The Real is not something behind the phenomenal world. It is what we apprehend in hope and humanity. If the distinction between nature and man is overlooked, determinism would be the universal rule.

Man, today, is suffering from a bewildering loss of community, a sense of alienation, an assimilation of the human being to a mass man, an organizational man in a technological society. Through a revolution in the conditions of life, man is becoming less and less human and therefore less and less free.

It is true that man has grown in the world of nature. Nature is the nourisher of the soul. After a billion years of life on this planet, only a few have seen the development of human ends and values. Man emerging from the slime, struggling against nature, against fellowman has his uniqueness. Though he rises from within nature man is different from what has preceded him in the evolutionary process. He is the first creature who has invented the future. He has developed a measure of freedom, of selfconsciousness, an aspiration to know the secret mystery of it all. Man, the thinker and the seeker, is an embodiment of the Divine. It is the spirit in him that sowed the seed, built the hut, rode the horse, launched the ship. Man built the great temples and cathedrals, he

[1] But I have that within which passeth show
These but the trappings and the suits of woe.

Hamlet, I. 2.

chiselled the great sculptures, drew the great paintings. It is, again, the spirit in him that launched the satellites which circle the earth according to the same laws of gravitation which govern the motion of the celestial bodies, the sun, the moon and the stars.

History is a matter of unique individuals involved in unique events. In it we find progress from the flint knife to the hydrogen bomb, from the cave to the skyscraper. God is the 'creator of creators'. The future is boundless and its possibilities unlimited.

Man is unique in being the one living creature, who is aware of his own existence as something possessing intrinsic significance. He does not treat life as meaningless. He acts on the assumption that the world has meaning or worth. He needs a faith by which to live. The religious instinct cannot be rooted out. If it is not satisfied with a given religion, it seeks an object elsewhere. In all religions there is faith, a desire to belong, a desire to escape from oneself.

In the drama of human existence we are both spectators and actors. Each individual is both I and me. The I should control the me. Indian thought, from the beginning of its history, has insisted on the method of meditation, of withdrawing from the 'me' and realizing the free spirit in man. It is not peculiar to Indian thought. Pythagoras told us, centuries ago, that different types of people went to the fair, a few to win laurels, some to do business, still others to see and watch. These last are the philosophers. In the same spirit, Plato describes a philosopher as the spectator of all time and existence. Pascal tells us that when the forces of the universe crush a man, they do not know what they are doing, but man knows that he is being crushed. This self-consciousness gives him dignity and freedom. If he overlooks this he lapses into routine, rigidity, mindlessness. The free detached spirit, which is not lost in the world of happenings, is responsible for the advances in art and literature, science and technology, philosophy and religion. When our lives are cluttered with possessions, and are spent in moving about in hectic hurry and noise, when in stress and strain, we find that our inward resources are depleted, and we turn to outward diversions, it is essential to emphasize the need for the contemplative spirit. It is those who stand outside history that make history.

It is wrong to think that we are in the grip of relentless determinism, and cannot alter the shape of things to come. The former Archbishop of Canterbury, Dr Fisher, expressed his opinion that it might be the will of God for man to destroy himself with atom bombs 'as he found nothing in scripture to suggest that the world would last for ever and much to indicate that it might not.' St Peter says that 'the heavens shall pass away with great violence, and the elements shall be melted with heat and the earth and the works which are in it shall be burnt up.' This counsel of despair suggests that man abdicates his responsibility and lets things drift. The abyss need not be our destiny.

The ethical basis of democracy is faith in the significance of man. The human person is not a mere wave on the ocean of history, which fancies that it pushes the flood while it is carried on by it.

We cannot disregard the impact of human initiative on human history. The great figures of history enter the exigencies of time and perceive what time had made ripe for development. They see what the world is ready for, grasp it and carry into existence what is in the womb of the past. Man can cause new currents to surge up in history. So long as personal responsibility and compassion are active in human souls, they will act and reshape human institutions, however venerable they may be with age.

III

No blind impersonal fate rules the world. Many people urge that it does not depend on individuals what the future of the world would be. In a complicated and highly integrated society, the individual loses his distinctiveness. If conflicts are caused, the governments are responsible and not the individuals. The peoples of the world have no quarrel with one another. The individual is not an abstraction. He is born a member of a group. Even when we do not like what the group does, we cannot escape responsibility for it.

The law of *karma* says that everything that happens, happens only because of the existence of antecedent causes and itself becomes the cause of subsequent effects. As we sow, so we reap. If there is no sowing there will be no reaping. This law holds in every sphere of life, physical as well as moral.[1] This view is not to be confused with predetermination.

[1] *cf:* Hobbes: 'Men heap together the mistakes of their lives and create a monster they call destiny.'

The laws of nature are necessary but the course of events is contingent. Modern mechanist societies lack the vision of the self in man. They recognize only an external mechanistic universe reflected in the machines that man has devised. This is how disintegration becomes the key image of the modern world. What we have done in the past has made us what we are now and gives us certain tendencies and latent dispositions, which we can alter by our effort. The past flows into the present. The future is what we choose to make of it. We are our own creators. This creative growth is possible only when we act as subjects and not objects. The carnal man remains always under the law; the spiritual man alone is capable of being born into freedom. We do not agree with the view of the depravity of man and the denial of free will. *Karma* is used to account for the conditions of life but man directs his destiny. We are weighed down by material ties and economic conditions crush us sometimes. Centuries of passions and systematized error have built a crust above our souls which light cannot pierce but the spirit when awake can produce miracles. Man's character is not formed solely by heredity and environment. He is free from such conditioning. If I may be forgiven for quoting myself, 'The cards in the game of life are given to us. We do not select them. They are traced to our past *karma* but we can call as we please, lead what suit we will and as we play we gain or lose. And there is freedom.'[1]

Even in history there is a strand of determinism. Our lives are inserted among necessities as the tree

[1] Radhakrishnan: *The Hindu View of Life* (12th impression, 1961) p. 54.

in the soil. The soil does not shape the foliage and the flowers. It is humanity and not the determined factors that shape the future. It is not necessary for us to assume that we can control things in an absolute way, that we are in the confidence of the Supreme, and that we can play Providence to the far future also. We overlook that human freedom has to reckon with brute malice or innocent miscalculation.

Each individual carries within himself two opposite instincts, the yearning for peace and the instinct for death. We should overcome the latter and unloose the knots of the heart, *hṛdayagranthi*. The free man is not one who sinks into a state of indifference or non-being, not one who gets beyond good and evil but one who is free from the obsessions of egotism and superiority. Man must tame himself. Morality is a continuous effort to bridge the gulf between personal claims and the law of morality.

There is a general view that God intervenes decisively in human history, revealing his own nature and enabling us to pierce our blindness, and overcome our weakness, so that we may become what we are meant to be, responsive to his love and doing his will. God is no arbitrary despot who denies the freedom of man. His power does not prevent us from being ourselves. He seeks to persuade rather than to compel. One of the instruments of his persuasion is the judgment that men bring on themselves if they persist in resisting the moral law but they remain free to resist. If we play recklessly with the means of our annihilation, it is not Divine responsibility. God does not threaten the humanity of man. The poet, in his drama, *Mudrārākṣasa*, makes Śiva, the master-dancer veil his devouring eye and guard his steps to save the world from plunging into the abyss. He achieves this aim through the minds and hearts of men. The course of history cannot be predicted, since human beings are not to be treated as measurable objects. They cannot be taken for granted.

Unfortunately the accumulation of scientific and technological possessions has deprived man of his inner freedom. We must seek ways and means to exorcize the demon of possessions, rescue man from his irresponsibility and make him the vital agent of civilization. The outward improvements do not touch our inner nature. Everything ultimately depends upon whether the man who is now such a great master of science and technology is also the master of himself. Our religions have not penetrated below the surface. The pressures of mass communication, the press, the radio, the television, tell us what we should think, what we ought to want and where to get it. Our community is a pressurized one. We think that we are enjoying new freedoms but pressures are stifling the spirit in us. Personal life becomes defunct. The mass society is the phenomenon which history has resulted in. Though pressed into a mass, the individuals are lonely and separate. Though living in an organized way, they have lost the sense of community. The despair and bewilderment of a generation gifted, insatiable, fanatic, with a sense of eventual doom, such a society is not the fulfilment of man. In it men are disoriented, obsessed and absurd.

A state of society like the one envisaged by

Aldous Huxley in his *Brave New World* or Orwell's *1984* which discourages the personal initiative of the human individual becomes a reality. It is the death of the human person that torments man. He follows the intuition of his heart when he abhors the total extinction of his own person. All the endeavours of technology, though useful in the extreme, cannot satisfy that desire for a higher life which is inescapably lodged in his breast.

Existentialism is a protest on behalf of the person against the mass and every tendency in our life to reduce the person to the status of a thing. The spiritual darkness can be overcome only by the recognition of the inherent dignity of man. Material welfare is not the only mark of civilized behaviour. A right to private life is the *sine qua non* of civilized beings. Man accepts responsibility for his actions because the Beyond is also within.

History is a series of conflicts, of moments when decisions have to be taken, though what decision we take depends to some extent on the exercise of freedom. The events in history are set in motion by the wills of individuals. A great man is great because he represents the will of the people. He is not an irrelevant epiphenomenon.

IV

What is the aim, the *telos* as the Greeks would call it, of human existence? Man's body is a perishable speck in the material universe; his mind is itself an instrument. The upward surge of nature cannot have body as its final product. There is something beyond, something that mankind shall be. The Eternal is in him but wrapped up in his constricted personality. Man's greatness is not in what he is but in what he can be. He has to grow consciously into it. His aspiration to participate in the divine creativity, his will consecrated to do so are the instruments of the evolutionary urge. Each individual has a specific role in the creative process. In the Viśiṣṭādvaita philosophy, the divine being and the human soul are one. There is one difference however. The Divine Lord has *Lakṣmī-patitva,* the lordship, mastery over *prakṛti,* over nature, while the human soul is lacking in this control of nature.

The Old Testament prophets believed that Yahveh, the God of Israel, would establish his kingdom over all the world. The view interprets history as the place where God works progressively towards an end. It accepts progress as the law of the cosmic process. There are many who believe that from generation to generation we are growing better. Lord Acton declared that without progress 'there is no *raison d'être* for the world'. For him to deny progress is to question divine government. We need not assume that the world gets worse and worse as time passes. Epicurus said centuries ago, 'We must remember that the future is neither wholly ours, nor wholly not ours: so that neither must we count upon it as quite certain to come nor despair of it as quite certain not to come'.

There is no inevitability of progress. Neither God nor Marxist dialectic gives us security about the future. Man can better himself through his own efforts, which are conditioned but not determined. History has a direction set with regard to certain fundamental characteristics by the dynamic mass of the past pushing it forward, but it is undetermined with regard to specific developments. Man with his freedom can triumph over the necessity in him.

We notice in history certain recurrent patterns or regularities; types of order into which phenomena fall. This is true of all fields of events. There are some recurrent features and also certain arbitrary inexplicable features. There are similarities and differences. Absolute similarity will reduce all differences to identity and there will be no meaning in comparisons. Absolute difference will eliminate all possibility of comparison. History exhibits some patterns but the details are not determined.

One of the deepest trends in human history is to escape more and more from submission to nature, stars or fate. Sartre points out that there are no links with the past in the making of new decisions. This is an overstatement. We cannot say that every decision is necessary. The free human being can quicken, stimulate, supersede, modify the process of nature or the growth of society.

Marx holds that the decisive element in human history is the material condition in which we work for our living. All else, philosophy, religion, politics are reflections or projections of underlying material relationships, of the techniques of production. A tribal agricultural society has a system of art and government which is different from that of a slave-owning society or a feudal one or a capitalist one. Each order of production gives way to its successor. Marx does not recognize that ideas working free from the restraints of fact bring about changes in the social order. With the passion of a Hebrew prophet Marx tries to bring down the mighty from their seats and exalt those of low degree. The ideals for which Marx and his followers fought and suffered are not just illusions on the surface of reality. The purpose of man is not material accumulation but the pursuit of art and culture. When we say that man is the high priest of nature, we affirm that he can do what nature cannot do. He can recognize nature's beauty, he can give voice to its magnificence. He can know the meaning of the world, understand his own past history, his relation to the animal kingdom as well as the forward movement of history.

New freedoms have been achieved by toil and effort. There is the extension of democratic equality, continual improvement in the conditions of labour. With the rise in the standards of living, with increased educational facilities, with decrease in the hours of labour, with a more comfortable and varied life, there are greater opportunities for reading and reflection, for leading illumined lives. Women, in many countries, have got rid of the restrictions of the past and have taken their place in every walk of life.

We realize the truth of our freedom only in moments of silence. The inventions and discoveries, the great revolutions, the visions and the prophecies all have their birth in moments of quiet. Thoughts that change the face of the earth are born in travail, in solitude. In such moments we feel the presence of the Unconditioned. It reveals itself in the finite texture of history. It saves the world from ultimate meaninglessness. Essential Being is brought into the world of existence. It is one of the paradoxes of religion that we have to raise the quality of life by renouncing self-interest.

With a sturdy belief in man we have to carry on our vocation. The sacred and the profane are intimately related. The saints transfigure life. They do not discard human nature or its values but plumb its depths. They are the mediators between heaven and earth.

There are moments in human history when, through lack of faith, lack of vision, man becomes identified with the frightening forces of chaos. The catastrophe which menaces us comes not from on high but from our own thoughts and ideals. If we submit passively to the forces we have raised, we are asking for destruction at our own hands. If there is one power that we possess, it is the power to alter our way of life. We should not resign ourselves to the march of time and forfeit our freedom but act as free creative beings, who, whatever the risks, are willing to assume the responsibility for the consequences of their acts. Our proneness to abdicate seems to be inexhaustible. We must recover our creative powers.

The pilgrimage of man is triumphant and heartrending by turns. In the new world which we have created for ourselves, we cannot cling to the old habits of mind. We should not persist in living in the ruins of the old world. The old man is on the way out. Man revolves on the wheel of hope and longing. The youth of the world has done nothing to bring about the present gruesome condition of things.

If we have a spark of love, a grain of intelligence we must protect the youth against the folly and stupidity of their elders. Our duty is to make an effort. It does not matter if we fail. It is better sometimes to fail than to succeed in doing harm.

History is the endless story of man's repeated failures. What commands our admiration is striving rather than success.

One version of the story of Pandora tells how Zeno gave man a cask filled with all good things; but man, beguiled by curiosity, lifted the lid, so that all the good things escaped to the gods, and as the lid was slammed down, hope alone remained captive and now consoles mankind. Man's history is a perpetual conflict between tragedy and hope.

The meaning of history is the transfiguration of life by those filled with holiness and humanity. They will bring about 'a new heaven and a new earth'.

The temporal being of the historical world will be taken over into the non-temporal mode of being of the Divine. History will move to its end and transform itself into the kingdom of spirit. The divine, working through god-men in the historical process, will lead to its deliverance, but not through a crisis or a catastrophe. The new man will be as different from the intellectual man as he is different from the animal being. These god-men pour fresh energy into the world and shape the whole course of mankind. Even when they are wayfarers within the world that passes, they have the eternal in them. Eternity is the fulness of time.

The spirit generated by truth is stronger than the force of circumstances. No other destiny awaits mankind than that which it prepares for itself through its own thinking and acting. There is no need to tread the path of decline to the end because what is in him is stronger than what is in the world. He can fling a flaming torch into the darkness of the future.

What is called *brahma-loka* by the Hindus is the Kingdom of God of the Christians. For St Paul Jesus is the earnest of the final redemption,[1] the pledge that the work of salvation already begun will be carried through to its consummation. His indwelling is the assurance of final resurrection.[2] The end of history is the final establishment of the Kingdom of God when God will be all in all.

Pascal in his *Pensees* observes that 'Christ will be in agony to the end of the world'. God is perpetual birth. It is ceaseless action. Till the end is accomplished, we have to strive onward. In this creative process, man is evolving into a higher species. He has to realize new possibilities. The cosmic process is unfinished.

[1] 2 *Corinthians* I. 22; V. 5.
[2] *Romans* VIII. 11.

CHAPTER VIII

THE WORLD COMMUNITY

I

The human race is involved in a new stage of history. Profound and striking changes are spreading over the whole world. These changes recoil on our thought and behaviour. The world is too small for nuclear weapons. They have to be brought under control in the interests of world community. A great cultural and social transformation is taking place. People are restless, alternating between faith and doubt, hope and anxiety.

In World War I, of the ten million people who were killed, 95 per cent. were soldiers and 5 per cent. civilians. In World War II, over fifty million were killed of whom 52 per cent. were soldiers and 48 per cent. civilians. In the Korean War, of the nine million killed, 84 per cent. were civilians and 16 per cent. soldiers. In these circumstances, it is difficult to believe that war that has degenerated into the mass murder of the defenceless, noncombatants, women and children, is a legitimate instrument of politics.

Nuclear developments have given enough power to the great countries to annihilate the human race many times over. Politicians have become indifferent to the growing danger and speak of balance of terror. The apathy of the masses and the indifference of the classes have resulted in a creeping paralysis of the people. If we do not wish to shut our eyes to the devastation which the building of nuclear armaments means, the destruction of cities, the ruin of countries, the sufferings of millions of human beings who are as good as ourselves, the demoralization of the world which acquiesces in a conspiracy of silence about the effects of nuclear explosions, the radio fallout, the annihilation of human beings, we must acquire a little quietude and think deeply. We should fight the immorality and unreasonableness which still govern the world. We must protest against the suppression of those who wish to enlighten the public about the realities of nuclear warfare. We should realize that there is no protection from nuclear weapons through shelters or emergency regulations.

In a world, where peace is becoming more and more precarious, the great powers have a special responsibility. With calmness, deliberateness and patience they have to face and meet problems. We need not assume that human nature is unchangeable and since there had always been wars, there would always be wars. World peace is not a dream in a shrinking world. It is a necessity, an essential condition for the survival of the human race. Can we attain this goal with the threat or the use of force?

William James in a famous essay on *The Moral Equivalent of War*[1] proposed a 'substitute for war's disciplinary functions'. He held out other ways of preserving martial virtues as 'the ideals of honour and standards of efficiency'. But it is not enough to propose equivalents for military virtues, we have to devise alternatives for the military methods. Issues which were hitherto decided through wars should hereafter be decided by other means. As long as there are nations, there will be disputes and they

[1] *1910.*

should be decided by peaceful means. In political life as in social life, we cannot exclude conflicts altogether. These have to be settled by a world organization, an international authority. Kant, in his essay on *Perpetual Peace* did not suggest a world state but a group of states, observing minimal rights of civilized behaviour. He proposed a notion of world citizenship, a common fabric of legal behaviour without the support of an overall sovereignty. The inter-penetration of states is the growing practice. World control by a single authority is an illusion. No democracy can become a world state. The latter may easily turn out to be a tyranny or a dictatorship. A federal solution is the way out, a world community which substitutes the processes of law for armed conflicts. The alternative to international anarchy is a world-wide system of justice, law and order. *Dharma* in Indian thought means a gathering in, a binding together, integration; *adharma*, its opposite, is a scattering out, a falling away, disintegration. The world has to be bound together. A world federal government with powers limited to those necessary for establishing and maintaining law and order among the nations of the world is a practical way of achieving just and lasting peace. Regional and political loyalties may stand against a world authority. We cannot abolish existing social structures without providing alternative ways of fulfilling functions discharged by them. We must have means to protect them against tyranny and aggression if they are not to submit to these evils. An international authority does not mean absence of wars. It will have coercive power to use, when necessary, against rebellious units. Within nation states we have rebellious citizens and groups, civil wars and revolutions.

The first world war was fought, to use President Wilson's words 'to make the world safe for democracy'. The League of Nations did not satisfy the American people who stood aloof from it.

A world authority to be effective is a consequence of a world understanding or world community. The present moral, social and political conditions of the world have to be altered before we can have a world community. We should work for a world community, for the alternatives are chaos or world tyranny.

II

From the beginnings of human history, poets, prophets and philosophers have asked us to grow equal to our destiny, to regenerate and transform ourselves by religious devotion, spiritual contemplation and moral courage. The Hammurabi code of the Babylonians, and the Egyptian Book of the Dead contain suggestions of the Ten Commandments of the Israelites. One of them reads 'Thou shalt not oppress the stranger for ye were once strangers in Egypt'. Hosea, Isaiah and Hillel emphasized compassion, mercy, forgiveness, piety and love. The prophet Isaiah states the promise of God. 'I will gather all nations and tongues; and they shall come and see my glory.'[1]

Alexander was struck greatly by the austerity of life and profound philosophic wisdom of the Indian teachers. He approached them without prejudice and acknowledged their greatness. Plutarch

[1] *Isaiah* LXVI. 18.

says that Alexander brought together into one body all men everywhere, uniting and mixing in one great loving cup as it were, men's lives, their characters, their marriages, their habits of life. He looked upon the whole inhabited world as his fatherland. All good men are of this; the wicked are the aliens. Aśoka, Harṣa and Akbar represent this view of life. Aśoka cut into rock the central lessons of the Buddha. By continually dwelling on the selfishness of others, we ourselves become more selfish. Not by accusing others do we get out of our selfishness but by purifying ourselves. The way from passion to peace is not by hurling charges against others but by overcoming oneself.

Jesus was trained in a context which could not accept the primitive morality of an 'eye for an eye'. For Jesus God was love and compassion as well as righteousness. 'Thou shalt love thy neighbour as thyself.' 'Return good for evil.' 'Bless those that curse you.'

Professor Max Mueller, who did a great deal for the interpretation of Indian religion to the western world, thought that he was a Christian Vedāntist even as some Christians are Christian Platonists. The aim of human existence was for him, as for many others, world community. 'Where the Greeks saw barbarians, we see brethren; where the Greeks saw nations, we see mankind, toiling and suffering, separated by oceans, divided by language, and severed by national enmity—yet evermore tending, under divine control, towards the fulfilment of that inscrutable purpose for which the world was created, and man placed in it, bearing the image of God.'[1]

[1] *Thoughts on Life and Religion*. An Aftermath from the Writings of Professor Max Mueller, by his wife, London 1905, p. 129 f.

Science has broken down the barriers of space and time. The independence of nations and the growth of the international community are felt the world over. The dream of conquering the vastness of space, of economic partnership across the frontiers of countries, of education for all our children, of employment for all who seek and need them are common to all.

The real force working for world unity is man's inborn compassion for others. It is the basis of life and requires to be organized. Our enemies are lack of courage, lack of imagination, indolence and inertia. We have to lead man towards civilization.

III

There is a deeper ethic, which calls every human being to eliminate the sources of conflict, the causes of war, to join with others to reform the institutions and relationships which lead to wars. Human reason and creative imagination should evolve the kind of education, mutual aid and collective security by which the nations will be able to resolve their differences peacefully. We should use cultural and ideological differences to enrich our wisdom and produce a higher international ethics.

The sovereignty of the world community comes before all others, before the sovereignty of classes and groups, tribes and nations. Every individual by his birth into the human family has the right to live and grow, breathe unpoisoned air and water on uncontaminated soil. Earth, water and air, now outer space and the celestial bodies are the common property of all mankind.

IV

The unification of the world is in process though it is struggling against many difficulties. Even as individuals are bound by the laws of the nation to which they belong, nation states should be bound by international law. Just as there are individuals who break the law, there are nations who break the law and commit aggression. The law of nations should be based on the federation of free states.

A society becomes cohesive if its members share large hopes, ideals and desires. If the world is to become a community, all the peoples should share common ideals and purposes even though they are separated by barriers, physical and psychological. All history is the story of remarkable individuals dramatically engaged in mastering the hostile environment. A few in every nation, in every part of the world, amid the uproar of nations and empires hear the voice of the future, the gentle stirring of life and hope. It is not one nation or one man. It is a new spirit that is awakened, revived and nourished by seemingly helpless but convinced and committed solitary individuals, to adapt the words of Albert Camus, whose deeds and works negate frontiers and breathe the oneness of humanity. As the result of their sufferings and sacrifices the vision of the threatened truth that each one of us belongs to the whole and should build for all becomes manifest. None of the differences which separate the governments of the world are as important as their membership in the family of nations.

The central problem is the development of loyalty to the world community. The greatest era of human history on earth is within reach of all mankind. To achieve this ideal, we have to discover our moral strength, define our purposes and direct our energies.

In facing this task, we come up against the crudest implications of history, that war is the maker of nations. Though, in previous epochs we waged wars which brought misery, destruction and ruin in their wake, we pointed out that defensive wars were better than shameful submission to barbaric aggressors who wished to achieve greatness and power by dominating the whole world. The two wars, the most ghastly in history, were waged by men of our generation. The leaders of the civilization who brought about these wars, in their moments of cool reflection, hate themselves for their responsibility. The world was full of oppressions and cruelties, stupidities and delusions and we thought we would remove them by resorting to violence. The nations today feel a genuine sense of guilt and shame. There is a widespread consciousness of the folly and wickedness in which most people and governments are involved. In spite of our earnest desire to get rid of wars, the fear of them, the baseness and savagery which that fear engenders are there raising the question, whether there is any hope for this perverted and criminal generation. Is there any hope that man can civilize himself? History is a dreadful warning. A few individuals suffer from mental derangements and some nations pass through nervous breakdowns resulting in excitement, violence and hatred.

The great powers are engaged in a struggle to capture the souls of the emerging peoples who have been released from colonial domination. These nations are in a state of inner turmoil. One conflict leads to another. Irrational feeling, racial hatred, primitive tribalism, poverty, hunger, suffering, intrigues, plots and counter-plots make of them a seething mass, mysterious and unpredictable. The new nations will have no peace, for the great powers are fighting on the soil of small emerging nations.

V

Our aim is to establish a world community based on a universal moral order.[1] It is possible only with a commitment to the ideal and practice of democracy based on the dignity of the individual. Even the most powerful nation or ruler must say with Shakespeare's Richard II:

> I live with bread like you, feel want
> Taste grief, need friends; subjected thus
> How can you say to me I am a king.

Democracy aims at achieving its ideals through persuasion, love, example and moral force. Violence and the machinery of intolerance are inconsistent with the spirit of democracy. The organizers of evil take a part of the blame and the many who acquiesce in it have to share a large part. We must emancipate human beings from the meshes they have woven round themselves, free them from the organizations of national selfishness. Even the fascist system claims to be democratic. Gentile, the Italian philosopher, sets forth the Fascist claim in

[1] *cf:* Professor W. E. Hocking: 'Religion . . . is the forerunner of international law because it alone can create the international spirit, the international obligation.' To this was added a footnote: 'We require a world religion just because we do not require, nor wish, a world state.' *The Meaning of God in Human Experience.*

these words: 'Democracy consists in giving the people what they want; they do not know what they want; the Leader tells them and then processes it for them.'

The United Nations Organization is the nearest we have to world government. It attempts to the best of its ability to eliminate the causes of conflicts. It affirms that international disputes should be resolved not by force of arms but by reasonable negotiations. It helps nations to remain in communication with one another for any co-operative or creative action. It uses moral force as a check on the aggressiveness and harassment of others. The United Nations Organization tries to free nations from political domination, racial oppression and economic exploitation. The right of a nation to survive depends not on the extent of its territory or the size of its population or its military might but its integrity and adherence to law. We aim at a family of nations to which each member will bring its unique gifts. All nations are sacred to themselves and so to each other and to the whole. The world should become an international commonwealth based on disinterested nationalism. Selfishness is sin whether in individuals or in nations.

Freedom from political exploitation is essential for human dignity. Freedom demands to be shared. The nation or the individual who enjoys freedom should make its bounds wider yet. Freedom is a spiritual quality. It overcomes all bounds and crosses all barriers. Freedom is universal in its application. Nationalism at one stage integrated people in Europe. The main spring of nationalism is the will of the people to be members of an independent sovereign state. Those who dominate other nations invent a thousand excuses for their conduct. They preach a doctrine of malice and intolerance towards the subject peoples. They carry a highly infectious disease which kills decent people. These merchants of hate drape themselves in a cloak of selfrighteousness. They exploit peoples' ignorance, prejudice and bigotry and destroy their ideals which they claim to uphold. Decolonization processes may be regarded as slow but they are steadily reversing the political subjection of peoples. It is no use telling people who are subjected to colonial domination that they are given education, health, the end of tribal feuds but in exchange they get humiliation.

Racial oppression is anti-democratic. There is only one race, the human race. It is above considerations of politics and nationality. Even the best of men subordinate racial evil to national interest.

Abraham Lincoln said, 'My paramount object in this struggle is to serve the Union, and is not either to save or to destroy slavery. If I could save the Union without freeing any slave, I would do it: and if I could save it by freeing all the slaves, I would do it; and if I could save it by freeing some and leaving others alone, I would also do that. What I do about slavery and the coloured race, I do because I believe it helps to save the Union; and what I forbear, I forbear because I do not believe it would help to save the Union. I have here stated my purpose according to my view of official duty; and I intend no modification of my oft expressed personal wish that all men everywhere could be free.' Civil rights are guaranteed in democratic constitutions. They imply the existence of an organized society maintaining public order without which liberty itself would be lost in the excesses of unashamed license. Every democracy should fight race discrimination.

Nationalism has lost its drive. The people of Europe wish to feel and think as Europeans. Many in Europe and other parts of the world hope to live under a universal system which no theorist foresees. More than half the population of the world suffer from hunger, malnutrition and disease. A world in which such things are permitted is a world of wilful insanity. We have brains to evaluate facts but we do not use them. Every area can be made fertile and habitable, every disease can be removed and every scarcity can be conquered. These are attempted by the Food and Agricultural Organization and the World Health Organization.

If a fraction of the expenditure we incur on armaments is diverted to social welfare we can clothe every man, woman and child and we will build schools for all of them. We will advance general health, housing, nutrition, culture and other ingredients of social well-being. This will help to eliminate fear, hatred and bigotry among nations. We will promote ethical enlightenment, spiritual freedom, development of artistic possibilities. We will live by sound reason and not by blind emotion or primitive instincts.

If the Communist faith has won the allegiance of millions of people, it is not because of their acceptance of Marxist theory but because of the sense of hope its gives to millions of its adherents by the advocacy of the overthrow of reactionary governments and the end of exploitation, racial, economic and political. It pleads for the economic progress of the common people, equality of economic opportunities. It attempts to abolish the distinction of rich nations and poor ones. It promises a rational allocation of resources and the establishment of world brotherhood. Those whose privileges and positions are challenged, are tempted to withdraw, emigrate inwardly to another state where they find security. The spread of communism has led to modification in the capitalist system and what was forecast as the inevitable collapse of capitalism did not happen. The system was greatly modified by the inspiration of communist doctrine or the trade union spirit. The middle classes did not merge into the proletariat but the latter rose to the rank of the middle classes. State Planning and the Government's responsibility for basic welfare became generally accepted. Technology made the workers not poorer but more prosperous.

We should wage a war against poverty. A true democrat should identify himself with the poor and the outcast. We must work for the social revolution.

VI

Men of imagination appreciate what is different from themselves. Homer and Shakespeare, St Paul and Francis are as much ours as Kālidāsa and Vālmīki. We are the heirs of all times and with all nations we share our inheritance.

The intellectually gifted are not ethically superior to the common people in the bitterness and injustice of their feelings. They are excellent as individuals but as members of groups they are as bad as others.

Even intellectuals are getting demoralized by accepting the view that truth is reached by statistical observations or empirical experiments. The pursuit of a meaning in life or purpose in conduct is dismissed as a romantic passion. They overlook that human beings have a conscience, have values, have imagination through which they create art and literature. If we wish to co-operate, we must learn about each other and each other's art and history. The UNESCO's range is wider. The artists, the thinkers and the scientists, whose works move multitudes, should know one another, understand one another and work together and lay the foundations for that great republic of beauty, truth and human brotherhood. We should work not only for our national aims, however just and reasonable they may be, but for the healing of discords of the political and economic world by the magic of that inward community of spiritual life which, in spite of difficulties, reveals to us our brotherhood and high destiny. Goethe said to Eckermann: 'As a man and a citizen, the poet will love his fatherland but the fatherland of his poetic powers and his poetic activity is the good, the noble, the beautiful which is the property of no particular person and no particular land. This he seizes upon and forms whenever he finds it.'[1] Gandhi says: 'I am wedded to India because I believe absolutely that she has a mission for the world . . . My religion has no geographical limits. I have a living faith in it which will transcend even my love for India herself.' 'I do not want my house to be walled in on all sides and my windows to be stuffed. I want the culture of all lands to be blown

[1] p. 91.

about my house as freely as possible. . . . But I refuse to be blown off my feet by any of them . . . Mine is not a religion of the prison-house. It has room for the least among God's creations. But it is proof against insolent pride of race, religion or colour.'

VII

There has been a steady progress in the democratic way, which is the way of non-violence. We were once cannibals, then we became nomadic hunters and later settled down to agriculture. These are signs of increasing non-violence and diminishing violence.

Great forces are at work bringing about a relaxation of tensions. These include the rising pressures in both democratic and communist countries for a more abundant life, the fear of mutual annihilation in a nuclear war, civilized leadership in the great countries. The whole direction of political society is towards freedom, the dignity of the individual and political democracy. Even totalitarian systems are moving relentlessly toward an open society. No dogma can for ever close the mind of the human being. The communist society is getting gradually democratized. The Soviet Union has passed through stages of development. It is capable of co-operating co-existence. Though the Communist States exploit revolutionary situations by the use of force, they do not rely entirely on force. Even this may disappear. Many States today need revolutionary changes for appeasing popular demands. Communism means modernization and a high degree of social justice. Stalin's Constitution of 1936 indicates a positive step in the direction of the recognition of human rights. In 1943, finding it difficult to uproot religion, the Soviet Union allowed the election of a Metropolitan of Moscow. Stalin announced that the party 'could no longer deprive the Russian people of their Church and freedom of worship'.[1] Envoys were exchanged with Western powers, with the United States in 1933. In 1945 the Soviet Union was a founder-member of the United Nations. If war is the breakdown of dialogue or conversation, to continue conversation is to accept the presuppositions of conversation, agreement, brotherhood and ethical principles. Dialogue or conversation means mutual understanding.

Rumania affirmed some years ago the right of each communist state to build socialism according to its own interests and desires. She is questioning the need for the Warsaw Pact, the military organization headed by the Soviet Union and comprising the six East European Nations including Albania. The French and the Rumanians both believe that times have changed since the two pacts were created, NATO in 1949 and the Warsaw Pact in 1955. Each country wishes to control its own forces. The Rumanian leader, Nicholae Ceausescu said on May 7 this year (1966) that the pacts were 'an anachronism incompatible with the independence and national sovereignty of the peoples and normal relations among States'. The Rumanians, a Latin nation in a Slav alliance, share President De Gaulle's view of a 'Europe of nations from the Atlantic to the Urals'.

[1] C. S. Braden: *War, Communism and World Religions* (1953), p. 260. Young men and women are seen today in Moscow wearing chains with crosses attached to them.

Eighteen years ago, Yugoslavia resisted Soviet domination. Marshal Tito is trying to free Yugoslavia from the shackles of party bureaucracy whose vision is narrow and to harness to the business of government and production new forces and new talents. He wishes to broaden the base of government by enlisting the active participation of men of ability, who have no use for party doctrine and intrigue. Yugoslavian society is opening to new ideals and influences. Yugoslavia and the Vatican have entered into an agreement and are exchanging envoys.

The Soviet Union and the East European States are becoming more nationalist and democratic. China is preparing for a new leap forward. Indonesia is attempting to have the rule of law and democratic government.

We do not have today capitalism or communism as we had in 1917. The changes taking place in them are necessary and convergent. The Communist states are striving to devise the right machinery for passing on power, for making a peaceful transition from one leader to another in a democratic way. When Mr Khrushchev was defeated in the party presidium, he appealed successfully to the party's Central Committee in June 1957. However, in 1964, he was made to retire.

After the war, we marched up to the brink in Greece and Turkey, Iran and Berlin, the Congo and Cuba. We marched down again. The signing of the Nuclear Test Ban Treaty is a step towards peace and away from war, towards reason. The combination of toughness and restraint saved the world. It is a hopeful sign that the Soviet Union has made proposals to the United Nations similar to those made by the United States in regard to the exploration of outer space.

International co-operation is accepted the world over. Woodrow Wilson, in his second inaugural address, said: 'The greatest thing that remains to be done must be done with the whole world for a stage and in co-operation with the wide and universal forces of mankind.'

We are conscious of living in a tragic age. We aim at lucidity and scepticism but hold our views with passionate intensity and enhanced sensibility. A truly religious man by his life and work sows the seeds of love and tolerance.

Our duty is to subdue the irrational and stabilize the international equilibrium. We are still growing, striving, looking confidently to an age when men will not be born into emptiness. The mantle of greatness belongs today not to those who make wars but to those who prevent wars. We must wake up into a world free of fear, myth and prejudice. Immediately after the Second World War, the East European States came under the influence of the Soviet Union. All of them adopted what is called a people's democracy, a one party system and the absence of civil liberties for the sake of the triumph of the proletariat. The countries of Western Europe, jealous of their freedom, sought the help of the United States. This entailed a relative loss of independence. The necessity of relative submission to the United States was felt to be humiliating and unwholesome and was resented by the former big powers, the United Kingdom and France and even the smaller ones with legendary memories of past history. Whenever danger arose and the Soviet Union intensified the 'cold war', the leadership of the United States became more pronounced. The Berlin blockade resulted in the Atlantic Pact. NATO's integration and the West German rearmament can be traced to the Korean War. The 'cold war' started between Soviet domination and the leadership of the United States.

VIII

India gained her independence in 1947 immediately after the second world war and, under the leadership of Jawaharlal Nehru, adopted the policy of non-alignment. A military approach is somewhat foreign to India. We are pledged to the principles of freedom and justice. The pursuit of peace, the liberation of subject peoples, the elimination of racial discrimination and international co-operation have been India's objectives. Any policy involving entangling alliances would have endangered Indian unity after independence, and would have made impossible the very limited economic development we have achieved.

This policy of peaceful co-existence is in accord with the spirit of India's genius:

ye yathā māṁ prapadyante
tāṁs tathai 'va bhajāmy aham
mama vartmā 'nuvartante
manuṣyāḥ pārtha sarvaśaḥ.[1]

'As men approach me, so do I accept them: men on all sides follow my path, O Pārtha (Arjuna).' Though beliefs and practices are varied, the goal of spiritual fulfilment is the same.

[1] *Bhagavadgītā*, IV. 11.

Aśoka in one of his edicts instructs those who were to carry the *dharma* to other countries: 'Remember that everywhere you will find some root of faith and righteousness, see that you foster this and do not destroy it.' He dreamed of the whole world to be federated by ideas, by the striving towards absolute truth and right conduct. It is the way to bind the diversity of races. His Rock Edict XII is an expression of this spirit:

'King Priyadarśī honours men of all faiths, members of religious orders and laymen alike, with gifts and various marks of esteem. Yet he does not value either gifts or honours as much as growth in the qualities essential to religion in men of all faiths.

'This growth may take many forms, but its root is in guarding one's speech to avoid extolling one's own faith and disparaging the faith of others improperly or, when the occasion is appropriate, immoderately.

'The faiths of others all deserve to be honoured for one reason or another. By honouring them, one exalts one's own faith and at the same time performs a service to the faith of others. By acting otherwise, one injures one's own faith and also does disservice to that of others. For if a man extols his own faith and disparages another, because of devotion to his own and because he wants to glorify it, he seriously injures his own faith.

'Therefore, concord alone is commendable,[1] for through concord, men may learn and respect the conception of *dharma* accepted by others.'

This spirit influenced Islam also. Abul Fazl

[1] *samavāya eva sādhuḥ*.

describes the spirit of Akbar's Universal Faith in these words:

'O God, in every temple I see people that seek Thee, and in every language I hear spoken, people praise Thee. Polytheism and Islam feel after Thee: each religion says, "Thou art One, without equal". If it be a mosque, people murmur the holy prayer and if it be a Christian Church, people ring the bell from Love to Thee. Sometimes I frequent the Christian cloister, sometimes the mosque. But it is Thou whom I search from temple to temple. Thy elect have no dealings with either heresy or orthodoxy for neither of them stands behind the screen of Thy truth. Heresy to the heretic; and religion to the orthodox. But the dust of the rose petal belongs to the heart of the perfume seller.'[1]

Rammohun Roy founded the Brahmo Samaj in the year 1830 and its trust deed contains the following:

'A place of public meeting of all sorts and descriptions of people without distinction as shall behave and conduct themselves in an orderly, sober, religious and devout manner for the worship and adoration of the Eternal, Unsearchable and Immutable Being who is the author and preserver of the Universe but not under or by any other name, designation or title peculiarly used for and applied to any particular being or beings by any man or set of men whatsoever.'

This spirit is opposed to the view that only one religion is valid:

'I am the Lord thy God . . . Thou shalt have no

[1] Blochmann, *Aini Akbari*, p. xxx.

other gods before me. Thou shalt not make unto thee any graven image, or any likeness of any thing that is in heaven above, or that is in the earth beneath, or that is in the water under the earth: Thou shalt not bow down thyself to them, nor serve them: for I the Lord thy God am a jealous God, visiting the iniquity of the fathers upon the children unto the third and fourth generation of them that hate me.'[1]

Non-alignment does not mean non-commitment. It is active commitment to peaceful co-existence, peace and disarmament. It gives freedom of action in international affairs. Non-alignment is not neutrality. Jawaharlal Nehru made this quite clear when he said at Columbia University, New York, October 17, 1949 that 'when man's liberty or peace is in danger, we cannot and shall not be neutral, neutrality then would be a betrayal of what we have fought for and stand for'.

We do not accept the thesis that every country has to choose one or the other group. The United States has a long record of non-involvement in other people's affairs. The foreign policy of the United States was for a century and a half dominated by President Washington's farewell address. He said:

'The nation which indulges toward another an habitual hatred or an habitual fondness, is in some degree a slave. It is a slave to its animosity or to its affection, either of which is sufficient to lead it astray from its duty and its interest.

'Europe has a set of primary interests which to us have none or a very remote relation. Hence she

[1] *Exodus* XX. 2 ff.

must be engaged in frequent controversies, the causes of which are essentially foreign to our concerns. Hence, therefore, it must be unwise in us to implicate ourselves, by artificial ties, in the ordinary vicissitudes of her politics, or the ordinary combinations and collusions of her friendships, or enmities. Our detached and distant situation invites and enables us to pursue a different course . . . Why by interweaving our destiny with that of any part of Europe, entangle our peace and prosperity in the toils of European ambition, rivalship, interest, humor or caprice? It is our true policy to steer clear of permanent alliances with any portion of the foreign world.'

Washington expressed his conviction that 'if we remain one people under an efficient government the period is not far off . . . when we may choose peace or war as our interest guided by our justice shall counsel.' Jefferson was only re-emphasizing this policy when in his first inaugural address on March 4, 1801, he advocated 'peace, commerce and honest friendship with all nations—entangling alliances with none'.

We have adopted the policy which was so well formulated by the leaders of the United States. A non-aligned country is not afraid to express its views. It is not neutral between good and evil, between right and wrong. Non-alignment is not isolationism. India participated in collective actions in Korea, Indo-China, the Middle East and the Congo. Non-alignment gives us the right, if not the authority, to influence the two great super powers.

The non-aligned nations which are not committed to either military group—communist or anti-communist—are unwilling to adopt an over-simplified attitude of black or white. They do not wish to divide the world into two camps—the wolves and the sheep. They recognize the intermediate shades and are willing to admit that both sides have elements of reason and justice. They also feel that the two systems are undergoing drastic changes. The Western powers are becoming more socialist in character and the Soviet Union is becoming more liberal in outlook. The United Kingdom, the Scandinavian countries and even the United States of America are not what they were at the beginning of the century. Lenin's Russia, Stalin's Russia and Khrushchev's Russia are different from one another. The Soviet Union has been changing from the old international ideal of World Communism to the government of a great power. At the time of the Russo-American rapprochement in 1959, Mr Khrushchev, forgetting for the moment his role as the leader of the world communist movement and speaking as a Russian said, 'if only Russia and America could agree, the peace of the world would be ensured, for between them the two great powers could stop any war anywhere'. Besides, there are different types of communism in Soviet Union, in China, in Poland and in Yugoslavia. Communist States are aiming at a radical liberalization of their regimes and the establishment of a new kind of socialist state. We must fight the ideologies which affirm the infallibility of their doctrines and divide the world into irreconcilable camps. The two systems have to live together if the threat of war posed by the nuclear and other weapons of mass destruction is to be removed. If the disarmament discussions are still continuing, it is because the great powers are increasingly aware of the dangers of nuclear war. We should try to increase confidence between nations. If we assume that war and capitulation are the only alternatives, it is due to the failure of imagination, to a sense of helplessness. We are so overwhelmed, even overawed, by the danger threatening us, that we have lost the capacity to think afresh and to act differently.

IX

International peace can be achieved by the self-discipline of sovereign States and not by the removal or abolition of States. We cannot have peace without law and law must be based on justice and not power. Only the spirit of justice can unite the whole human race. Through the gift of patience, spiritual wisdom, we should show the way to the solution of the problem which faces all the peoples of the world. In spite of racial and national differences, we must evolve a relationship, a unity of mind and heart, a feeling which will bring us intimately close to one another. We must strengthen the forces of sanity in society. Every truly religious man whose nature is freed from dogmatic rigidity realizes that all prayers flow into one Supreme. We must create new men who will stay our doom, and build a new humanity. It is inevitable that a new spirit of oneness will take hold of the human race. Wars and revolutions may retard but the final unification is clear. Nations should progress slowly to remove the barriers that separate them and test each other's sincerity at every step so that in time mutual confidence is created.

World government may be a long way off but we must continue at an ever increasing rate to blunt the edges of national sovereignty. Nations should compete peacefully with one another in establishing the reign of truth and justice. This has to be done with effort.

We should free the concept of the Divine from all objective and anthropomorphic attributes. Man becomes aware of his potential identity with the Divine. Hindu thought emphasizes the importance of the divine character of the human being—*tat tvam asi*—that art thou. The Boddhisattva, the nature of enlightenment is in all. Jeremiah's last words are to the effect: 'I will put my law in their inward parts, and write it in their hearts; and will be their God and they shall be my people.'[1] Christianity which affirms, 'Behold, I make all things new', uses the concept of the Holy Spirit as 'the spirit of truth', 'the bearer of witness' and 'the promise of the Father'. 'The Kingdom of God is within you.'[2] 'The truth shall make you free.'[3] 'The true light which lighteth every man that cometh into the world.'[4] 'God is a spirit: and they that worship Him must worship Him in spirit and in truth.'[5] In Christian theology the emphasis is on God the spirit. It is this that is manifesting itself in the strivings for peace, the struggle for civil rights and social justice by men of all faiths.

The knowledge of God in the human being is

[1] *Jeremiah* XXXI. 31–33.
[2] *St Luke* XVII. 21.
[3] *St John* VIII. 32.
[4] *St John* I. 9.
[5] *ibid.* IV. 24.

possible through the withdrawal of the senses and mind from the world of outer experience and concentrating these energies on the inward reality. Man realizes his true nature through this inward penetration. When the individual gains the knowledge of the self, he becomes illumined, the bonds of the heart are destroyed, and his finiteness is transcended.

The discipline of religion is to make this potential into actual. This identification of the Divine is not a matter of history but of personal experience of the individual. At the centre of our being we encounter a world where all things are at rest and the differences which divide us fade into insignificance. This experience is through the cultivation of man's inward life. Man has to devote himself for a few minutes each day to the best that is in him. We must cleanse the soul of self-delusion. Until the human individual explores the contents of his consciousness and with deliberation and effort makes himself one with the Divine and affirms with conviction, 'I and my Father are one', the Divine is transcendent, the 'wholly other'.

In our conduct of affairs the effect of unreason is so obvious that mind itself becomes a wilderness. 'Wrath is cruel and anger is outrageous.'[1] Thomas Jefferson wisely counselled 'when angry, count ten before you speak, if very angry, an hundred'. We should bring our temper under control before it blazes forth in harsh words and unjust accusations, before our excited emotions make it difficult for us to judge wisely. We must develop self-control through brotherly love which confers a tranquil frame of mind that is difficult to overthrow. If we

[1] *Proverbs* XXVII. 4.

take man as he is, we will be in despair; if we take him for what he ought to be, we will help him to become that. Man's understanding of himself leads to a life of disciplined disinterestedness and of love for all. The brotherhood of man is a present possibility. New men with a new instinct to unify, to share, serve and sacrifice are possible. If mankind is released from the pressure of population, if the waste of warfare is avoided, if the sources of wealth are organized by the community, people will become free and adventurous and not lead lives of routine and indolence.

In man and his future we must have confidence. The ideal of world community, our obvious destiny and duty, is at once a summons to creative endeavour, and a call to co-operative action.

INDEX

Index

Index

Index

GEORGE ALLEN & UNWIN LTD.

London: 40 Museum Street, W.C.1

Auckland: P.O. Box 36013, Northcote Central, N.4
Bombay: 15 Graham Road, Ballard Estate, Bombay 1
Barbados: P.O. Box 222, Bridgetown
Buenos Aires: Escritorio 454–459, Florida 165
Calcutta: 17 Chittaranjan Avenue, Calcutta 13
Cape Town: 68 Shortmarket Street
Hong Kong: 105 Wing on Mansion, 26 Hancow Road, Kowloon
Ibadan: P.O. Box 62
Karachi: Karachi Chambers, McLeod Road
Madras: Mohan Mansions, 38c Mount Road, Madras 6
Mexico: Villalongin 32–10, Piso, Mexico 5, D.F.
Nairobi: P.O. Box 4536
New Delhi: 13–14 Asaf Ali Road, New Delhi 1
Ontario: 81 Curlew Drive, Don Mills
Rio de Janeiro: Caixa Postal 2537–Zc–00
São Paulo: Caixa Postal 8675
Singapore: 36c Prinsep Street, Singapore 7
Sydney, N.S.W.: Bradbury House, 55 York Street
Tokyo: P.O. Box 26, Kamata

Other books by Sir S. Radhakrishnan

EAST AND WEST IN RELIGION

'Full of mental nourishment and moral stimulus.'
Aberdeen Press and Journal

'Amplifies the idealist view of life . . . set forth in his Hibbert lectures.' *Sheffield Daily Independent*

'Will bring illumination to all who read it.' *News Chronicle*

'The book grows on the reader as he reads . . . This is a great work, which will stand the test of time, and can be recommended to any seeker after truth. The publishers are also to be congratulated on the good appearance of the book, its style and finish.' *Everyman*

'Written with the author's usual distinction of style, and is only too short, not for his purpose, but for the readers' appetite.' *Manchester Guardian*

RELIGION AND SOCIETY

'The product of a deeply religious mind, able to bring timeless value to bear upon world events, and thus to strength, faith and hope in the act of being bleakly realistic about the dangers and corruptions of the present.' *British Weekly*

'Professor Radhakrishnan's work is the fruit of deep religious conviction and a fine philosophical intellect equally at home in East and West.' *The Guardian*

'A highly stimulating and deeply satisfying book. If one wishes to see the great problems that face mankind today through the eyes of one steeped in both the wisdom of the East and the philosophy of the West, there is probably no-one more competent to give us that insight than Professor Radhakrishnan.' *Inquirer*

'A book to ponder over . . . at once a call to further endeavour, and, in its faith in the future spirituality of man, a promise of beauty as exhilarating as the beauty of a work of art.' *Oriental Art*

INDIAN PHILOSOPHY

'This book marks an epoch in speculative thought. It is probably the first important interpretation of the Eastern mind from within.' *Glasgow Herald*

'The first volume takes us to the decay of Buddhism in India after dealing with the Vedas, the Upanishads, and the Hindu contemporaries of the early Buddhists. The work is admirably done.' *Nation*

'In this very interesting, lucid and admirably written book . . . the author has given us an interpretation of the philosophy of India written by an Indian scholar of wide culture.' *Daily News*

'It is among the most considerable of the essays in interpretation that have come from Indian scholars in recent years. English readers are continually on the lookout for a compendium of Indian thought written by a modern with a gift for lucid statement . . . Here is a book for them.' *The New Statesman*

'We are fortunate in that Professor Radhakrishnan is evidently deeply read in the philosophy of the West, and shows considerable acquaintance with general Western literature; a happy blend of Eastern conceptions with Western terminology makes the book intelligible even to the inexpert, and, it need hardly be added, instructive.' *The Times*

'A work of feeling as well as of lucid thought. An exposition of living interest. The author is to be congratulated on the a solid piece of work.' *The Spectator*

'This remarkable and learned work . . . we welcome it as a significant sign of our times.' *The Birmingham Post*

'An intellectual achievement of the first rank, and may be regarded as authoritative.' *The New Statesman*

'The spirit and motive and method of this great book are admirable . . . a real contribution to the unification of the mind of humanity through mutual understanding.' *The Church Times*

'A very considerable achievement.' *Theology*

'A storehouse of learning for those who are interested in world philosophy.' *Holborn Review*

THE BHAGAVADGITA

'He provides not only a Sanskrit text and English translation but an illuminating introductory essay and notes suggesting parallels to its teaching not only in Eastern but in Western writings . . . this edition may help us to understand not only what the writer of the *Gita* taught but what that teaching means to the most distinguished exponent of Neo-Hinduism who once more reveals the astonishing range of his reading and his gift of bringing, if not into unity yet into association, ideas derived from very different sources.' *Congregational Quarterly*

'Wide scholarship and mature thinking meet one both in introduction and in the commentary . . . the Introduction and light commentary on the *Gita* has the hallmark of fluent exposition, genial reasonableness and great scholarship without pedantry, all of which we expect from Dr S. Radhakrishnan. The Hindu, the Indian Christian, the Western Christian and the scholar seeking to understand the Gospel of Hinduism will find in this book a trustworthy guide speaking to them in a language and ideas they are able to understand and appreciate.' *The Guardian, Madras*

'Will hold its own as the best work of this class in English. Preceding the text and translation is an Introductory Essay of over sixty pages in which with admirable conciseness the philosophy underlying the Bhagavadgita is set forth. The Sanskrit text is given in Roman script, and each stanza with its translation is followed by an illuminating, interpretative notes, all the more interesting for the wide range and variety of the allusions and references in them.' *Philosophy*

'This is a distinguished book . . . Its stimulating, scholarly, and sympathetic approach deserves wide recognition . . . a translation that is a triumph of clarity, ease, and plain honesty. It is beautiful, and the arrangement ideal. For the Sanskrit precedes the translation, this in its turn followed with comparatively few exceptions by some explanatory comment or some reference to other works.' *The Theosophical Forum*

THE HINDU VIEW OF LIFE

To the west religion in India tends to appear as a rich and rather baffling tangle of myths, with endless gods and goddesses worshipped in countless different forms. But this complexity, which springs as much from an exuberant love of story-telling as anything, is only the surface of Indian faith. Underlying it is a system of unifying beliefs that have guided the ordinary Indian family for thousands of years, and provided inspiration for many other oriental peoples.

These are here set forth with the clear ease and authority of one of the profoundest philosophers of east or west.

Unwin Book

THE BRAHMA SŪTRA

The Philosophy of Spiritual Life

The illustrious scholar-statesman Dr Radhakrishnan to whom we already owe many standard works on religion and philosophy, here gives us another classic. The spiritual tradition of India is based on the three-fold canon *prasthāna-traya,* the *Upaniṣads,* the *Bhagavadgītā* and the *Brahma Sūtra.* These texts are not only bound up with a historic past; they are a living force in the present and have a contemporary accent. Though the conditions of modern life have become different and are in some ways better, we cannot say that we are superior to the ancients in spiritual depth or moral strength. The problems which the *Brahma Sūtra* raises and attempts to solve are not dissimilar to those which engage us even today, the nature of the Supreme Reality, the status of the world, the future and destiny of the individual, the pathway to perfection.

This study of the *Brahma Sūtra* is a notable contribution to the development of solidarity in thought to which our world is committed. It is no exaggeration to say that this book in its theme and in its serene prose will prove invaluable to all those who are interested in the problems of man's spiritual quest and fulfilment. A book of the highest erudition and authority.

AN IDEALIST VIEW OF LIFE

'Science is a system of second causes, which cannot describe the world adequately, much less account for it.' Anybody who has felt this, however vaguely, will find in Dr. Radhakrishnan a rich source of nourishment. He first examines the modern intellectual ferment, and the vain attempts to find a substitute for religion. He then discusses, drawing with equal ease on thinkers of east and west, the nature and validity of religious experience. Finally, he creates a fine vision of man's evolution, and the continuing emergence of ever higher values. The wealth of material, together with the author's own living faith, undogmatic and demanding no creed, make the book a complete philosophical education in itself. *Unwin Book*

THE RECOVERY OF FAITH

In this inspiring book, one of the most brilliant of modern philosophers and statesmen gives an answer to man's need for a new faith. In examining the creeds men have lived by in the past and present, Dr Radhakrishnan covers in simple style a great variety of religious thought, from the ancient Upanisads to the ideas of William Penn and our own times in the persons of Sartre, Bergson and others. He exposes the pretensions of communism and explores the inner meanings of Hinduism, Judaism, Christianity, Taoism and other beliefs. He shows how, out of these enduring spiritual expressions, a religion can be achieved which will satisfy humanity's aspirations by transcending dogmatic and sectarian differences.

The World Perspective Series